# Teens Write Through It

# Teens Write Through It

## ESSAYS FROM TEENS WHO HAVE
## TRIUMPHED OVER TROUBLE

*Compiled by the editors at Fairview Press*

## Fairview Press
### MINNEAPOLIS

Published by Fairview Press, 2450 Riverside Avenue South, Minneapolis, MN 55454.


**Library of Congress Cataloging-in-Publication Data**

Teens write through it : essays from teens who have triumphed over trouble / compiled by the
    editors at Fairview Press.
        p.     cm.
     Summary: Essays by teens about how they dealt with such problems as drug addiction,
sexual abuse, disability, racism, divorce, anorexia, and depression.
      ISBN 1-57749-083-5 (alk. paper)
      1. Youth--United States--Case studies.   2. Courage--Case studies.  3. Adjustment
(Psychology)--Case studies.  [1. Interpersonal relations.   2. Conduct of life.   3. Courage.
4. Children's writings.   5. Youths' writings.]   I. Fairview Press.
HQ796.T4135   1998
305.235'0973--dc21                                98-35997
                                                                CIP
                                                                AC


First Printing: September 1998

Printed in the United States of America

02  01  00  99  98     7  6  5  4  3  2  1


Cover: Cover Design by Laurie Duren


Publisher's Note: Fairview Press publications, including *Teens Write Through It*, do not necessarily reflect the philosophy of Fairview Health Services.

For a free current catalog of Fairview Press titles, please call toll-free 1-800-544-8207. Or visit our website at www.Press.Fairview.org.

# Contents

# Racism

# Family Trouble

# Body Image

# Immigrant Experience

# Depression

## MOVING

## DIFFICULT CHOICES

## RELATIONSHIPS

## SELF-ESTEEM AND OTHER NEW PERSPECTIVES

## Sexual Assault

## Death and Dying

# Foreword

FOUR YEARS AGO, AMID A DELUGE OF HEADLINES FILLED WITH alarming statistics and dire predictions about our nation's youth, Fairview Press launched its own mission of hope based on a simple premise: If you want to know the truth about something, go to the source. It sponsored an essay contest for teens ages twelve through nineteen (I was privileged to have served as one of the judges) and subsequently published the winning entries in the book *From Darkness to Light: Teens Write about How They Triumphed over Trouble*. The goal was not to negate the challenges and struggles of contemporary adolescence, but to focus on the inspiring strength of spirit that drove each of the writers to overcome adversity rather than surrender to despair.

As the former Coordinator of Young Adult Services for the Minneapolis Public Library and a lifelong youth advocate, I have not only worked with many teens throughout the years, but also facilitated numerous workshops for adult professionals in libraries throughout the region. I have learned how critical adults are in the lives of adolescents, regardless of appearances, and how vital it is that we listen to adolescents with respect and good humor—a point well supported by research, particularly the Search Institute's landmark study on developmental assets.

I cannot count the number of times I have walked into a classroom, my cart full of magazines and books in tow, and seen apathy or bravado transformed into rapt attention and fascinating dialogue. I have learned that kids think about a great many things, from their personal relationships and place in the world, to the fate of the earth and humanity. While I enjoy the often lively debate and commentary that can take place in a classroom environment, I have learned the most from the many teens who have sent me a note or pulled me aside to ask a question. It is then that I see the greatest vulnerability, deepest emotion, and strongest empathy reveal itself beneath what is often typical adolescent posing. I am, at times, profoundly moved to realize just how much of a difference even a brief meeting can make.

When I work with adults, I always ask how many of them would return to their adolescence if they could. The response has been consistent. (I think only one hand rose up during the countless programs I've presented, and that one rather tentatively.) This is the most important reminder I can give to any adult who interacts with teens: Place yourself back in those shoes and remember.

Adolescence has always been a hellish time, generating a sense of isolation and self-consciousness that make it particularly crucial to reach out and communicate, and it has only gotten harder over the years. As Patricia Hersch states in her book, *A Tribe Apart: A Journey into the Heart of American Adolescence:*

> *". . . the [very] fabric of adolescence has changed. . . . Today's teens have grown up in the midst of enormous social changes that have shaped, reshaped, distorted, and sometimes decimated the basic parameters for healthy development. Sometimes the experience is positive . . . but too often these days the results can be negative, irreversible, even deadly."*

And yet, according to a recent *USA Weekend* poll of almost 300,000 teens, only one-third of the respondents reported talking to a parent more than fifteen minutes a day, while another third said they rarely or never speak with a parent at all.

The implications of these two observations are staggering. Never has it been more critical to provide a forum for teens to express themselves and connect with the larger universe. While the pressures of growing up are greater than ever, the need to define and anchor oneself in a rapidly changing and unpredictable universe is still at the heart of adolescent development and growth.

That is why I am so excited to see this new edition of teen writing from Fairview Press. Once again we journey with teens through their personal heart of darkness—whether it involves drugs or addiction, gangs and violence, grief or depression, disability or disease—and emerge with them into the light of hope and healing.

In the essay, "Don't be Afraid to Say No," a Kimberly Agnew writes a letter to drugs, which were once her "best friends." When she writes, "I want you out of my life . . . you did nothing but hurt me more than I was already hurting . . . I wish you were gone, but you never will be, because I will always have my memories," we know just how difficult her struggle has been—and continues to be—to abandon this relationship. When Kiersten Johnson, the author of "My Story," tells us how, since the age of four, her numerous bouts with cancer and other devastating illnesses have culminated in her most recent diagnosis at age sixteen, this one offering no hope, we are humbled by her final words: "Live your life to the fullest! . . . Be yourself! Take a moment to look around at this wonderful world! Take time to visit the people you mean to visit 'one day,' because you never know when you will be one day too late." We are chilled and deeply saddened by Maria Caballero's horrifying description of her rape in "The Nightmare": "His hands were all over her body . . . it was like a rose . . . getting ripped from its bush, tearing her hopes and dreams out of reality."

Each story in this book bristles with the raw and brutal honesty of a young writer struggling down the path toward growth and personal redemption. As Danny Young describes his transition to a new country and new language in "My Life," he captures the essence of every story in this collection with these insightful words: "The day came when the risk it took to remain tight inside the bud was more painful than the risk it took to blossom."

I invite you to meet the courageous teens introduced in these pages who, through their willingness to share with us their deepest vulnerabilities and personal pain, offer the strongest rebuke to chilling headlines of violence and rage. Their voices speak for the many who represent our greatest hope for tomorrow.

ADELA PESKORZ

*Adela Peskorz is the Assistant Librarian and Instruction Coordinator at Metropolitan State University. Her many years as a professional Young Adult Specialist and advocate have left her with an exuberance and enthusiasm for working with young adults.*

# Preface

WHEN WE SPONSORED OUR FIRST TEEN WRITING CONTEST FOUR years ago, we had hoped to provide a forum for young people to discuss how they had overcome difficulties in their lives. We had also hoped that the writing process itself might become part of the healing process. But we had not anticipated how these young writers would inspire so many other people—both young and old—to maintain their courage in times of trouble, to survive, and, ultimately, to grow.

Last year we announced our second writing contest, and the response has been overwhelming. Hundreds of essays have poured in from across the nation. Many of these essays were heartbreaking to read; all were inspirational. We were deeply moved by the extraordinary courage and resiliency of these young writers, and we applaud their success in the face of adversity.

These essays are not sugar-coated; they are blunt, brutal, and bold. All speak about the troubling issues that affect young people today. Sexual assault, drug abuse, death, illness, racism, loneliness, body-image—they're all here.

In the winning essay, "Wrong Sex, Wrong Color," Rayvon Scott describes the humiliation that he and his friend experienced when they were confronted by a police officer as they played with their white friend's young children. "We had been violated and disrespected . . . we felt like we really had committed a crime." He writes not only of his anger and his pain, but of his sincere "wish for people to see that black and white aren't the only colors in the rainbow, and that not all things that are different are wrong."

In the second-place essay, "Escape," Patty Vodenka tells a remarkable tale of family cohesion, perseverance, and courage as she takes us back to 1983, when she and her family escaped then Communist Czechoslovakia. "My heart was pounding, my chubby legs running as fast as a four-year-old's could. . . . Flashlights from behind us and gunfire in front of us lighted our way. I could hear feet splashing through the puddles . . . dogs barked. . . . We kept running into the darkness, not knowing how far we had gone, how far we had to go. Not knowing if they were going to catch or shoot us, like so many they had caught and killed before us."

The third-place essay, by Gianna Cardinale, describes a most amazing turnaround. "Challenging Anorexia" takes us to hell and back through the author's painful struggle with her eating disorder. "I vaguely remember coming home each day, sitting in front of the fire, scorching my paper-thin skin and scalding my untasting mouth with boiled tea in an attempt to keep warm. My nails grew thin and brittle, my hair thinned and receded, and a disgusting fuzz grew all over my bony body (a natural reaction by the body in an effort to keep warm). One night, I woke up with my mom huddled around me. She was afraid my heart would stop in my sleep."

Every writer in this book has a story to tell. They have confronted their challenges head-on, and they have found the courage to write honestly about their experiences and share them with the wider world. They have persevered through dark times and emerged with strong, courageous voices. They have triumphed over the trouble in their lives. Let these young people be an inspiration to us all.

FAIRVIEW PRESS

# Acknowledgments

FAIRVIEW PRESS WOULD LIKE TO THANK THE FOLLOWING ORGANI-
zations for their gracious support of this project. Without them,
this book would not have been possible.

For their generous financial sponsorship, we would like to
thank the Fairview Foundation. We would also like to thank:

Automated Mailing Corporation
Capital City Pride
Cold Side Silkscreening
DRAGnet
Hungry Mind Bookstore
Mall of America
Message! Products
Minnesota Vikings
Simek's
Soderberg Florist
SuperAmerica
Tiro Industries
Walgreens

For her special contribution to this project, we sincerely thank
Adela Peskorz.

We would also like to thank our panel of judges, whose time and effort has contributed so much to the finished product of this book:

Mayor Sharon Sayles Belton of Minneapolis
Marly Cornell, Fairview Health Services
John Edwards, Adoptive Families of America
Senator Rod Grams of Minnesota
Linda Hillyer of Minnesota
Nkauj'lis Lyfoung, KTCA's *Don't Believe the Hype*
Rosemarie Park, University of Minnesota
Mark Vukelich, Fairview Health Services
Senator Paul Wellstone of Minnesota


Finally, for the heart behind the book and the words within each story, we would like to thank all the young people who sent in their essays. Though the final choices for publication were difficult, every essay we received contributed to this remarkable book. Thank you all, from Fairview Press.

# DRUGS AND ALCOHOL

# I've Found
# the Ultimate High

........................

*GAB, age 16*

AT A TIME WHEN MOST PEOPLE MY AGE WERE BEGINNING TO THINK about their future, I chose to explore being a druggie.

If I decide that something is worth doing, I do it all out. That's simply my personality. So when I started doing drugs, I went all out.

It started, as it usually does, with smoking pot. On my fourteenth birthday, my boyfriend gave me a dime bag of opium-laced weed. After that first bowl, all I wanted to do was find a high. I bought *The Basketball Diaries* and dreamed of the day when I could move out of my parents' house and become a heroin junkie. My drug use quickly accelerated, and I began to concentrate on harder drugs (in keeping with my all-out personality). As my friends were growing up, I was growing mushrooms and certain pharmaceuticals. I was a good druggie.

During my sophomore year in high school, I found my new best friends in powders. I drank, snorted cocaine, and shot up heroin and crystal meth. I became the druggie of my dreams.

On the last day of tenth grade, I decided that I deserved a little vacation. I stayed in town for a week, doing speed with my friends. I didn't eat or sleep for seven days. My family had no idea where I was, and they were frantic. Eventually, my mother took to driving around town. She found me on a muggy Tuesday afternoon. When she saw me, she broke down sobbing in the driver's seat of her car. I had been wearing the same clothes for a week, and I had taken only one shower. (I couldn't stand the thought of water while I was on speed.) I hadn't eaten, either. Food and meth do not mix—you have to choose between puking sick or hollow and hungry. I chose hungry.

Since then, I have tried to put myself in my mother's place—frantic, sleepless, worried, imagining the worst. She found her baby on the streets, strung out, dirty, hungry, and lost. She burst into tears when she saw me and begged me to come home with her. I looked her straight in the eye and said, "I have things to do tonight. I can meet you here at two o'clock tomorrow." Then I turned and walked away. I can't imagine the pain my mother felt as she watched me step back into the shackles that drugs had placed on my soul.

I went into treatment the next day and stayed for almost two months. When I left, I was on Step Ten of the Alcoholics Anonymous Twelve-Step Program. I had planned out my life for the next ninety years. I was on a huge treatment high.

After two weeks, however, the novelty of sobriety wore off. A friend I had met in treatment called to say that she had run away. I told her to come over and stay the night.

She drove to my house that afternoon. I had to go to work, so she went to the county fair and arranged to pick me up when I got off. We met at around midnight and I took her on a tour of my town. We ended up getting stoned at an old buddy's house. I had fifty-eight days clean and was looking forward to my next sixty. I never saw it.

The next day, we took off. We waited until my mother had left for the day, threw all of my things in her trunk, and drove. I felt sick leaving my driveway. I didn't want to go—I had been doing so well. But I had gotten stoned, and the little druggie in me said, "Give it your all!" So I did.

We ended up in Texas, smoking crack, heroin, PCP, and the best weed in the world. I started to feel tough. I considered myself a jaded cynic; I had seen it all through stoned eyes. Nothing could touch me. I told one of the men we were staying with that "I really knew how to party." I was a little sixteen-year-old girl from Minnesota; these people were Crips, raised in the 'hood, with gold in their teeth and guns in their pockets. I thought I was tough—they proved that I wasn't.

The last night of my adventure started out with crack and gin and juice. It ended with me shaking on the bed, in the throes of overdose seizures, sobbing because I would never see my mommy again. Those two gang-bred, cruel-hearted crack dealers helped themselves to something sacred, and I was left naked on the bed, a scared little girl hoping her death would be painless and quick.

That night, life showed me what I was. I had to learn an all-out, big-time lesson to see that I was killing myself with my all-out, big-time habit. I was just a little girl, doing more drugs than any sane person could handle. I played with fire until I got burned badly enough to realize the fatality of my toys.

Staying off drugs isn't a huge problem. The tenacity that taught me to hold on to the drug life is helping to keep me away from it. I stay clean by following what I know. I listen to my mind. The power of the mind is infinitely greater than the power of any drug. I focus on my good traits instead of my shortcomings. I live life like anyone else; I just don't do drugs. If I go to a party, I pass the bowl to the next person. Drugs are no longer a factor in my life.

I enjoy being clearheaded. I revel in the fact that I can get up in the morning and make my bed. I get a rush from being responsible, doing what I ought to do. The person that once needed to live life at three hundred miles per hour has found contentment in sitting still. I'm riding in the backseat now, letting the Powers That Be run things. I didn't do such a great job when I was driving.

Over the past few years, I have learned many things. Drugs are fun, I'll be the first to admit that. But tasting and experiencing this weird reality of life gives me a bigger rush than I ever found in drugs. After years of searching for the ultimate high, I have found it. My high lies in living, and it's the best high anyone could ever experience.

# My Drug Life

*Rachel E. Fesenmaier, age 15*

IT ALL STARTED IN THIRD GRADE. I STARTED OUT ALONE, BY myself, with no one to turn to. My dad was demanding and cruel. My mom followed his steps and did what he wanted her to do and never cared about herself. My sisters moved away and started a new life. My brother was becoming just like my father, but stronger. And then there was me, the young one who couldn't handle anything and never did anything right.

There were no smiles in our house, no comfort, no love. The worst time of the day was when it came time to eat a meal. My father would go around the table and say how crappy we were and how we screwed up everything. My father would beat us if we didn't do what we were told or if we made a mistake. At the end of fifth grade, my father molested me. I kept it inside, and from then on he acted as though I was his child and his alone. I felt alone and ashamed. After a couple months, my brother and I started hanging around each other a lot. I became a tomboy.

My dad raped me behind the wall of the top stairs. He covered my mouth with pressure and was very forceful. He continued that for awhile. After a time, I never thought anything of it. It was natural and I let him hurt me.

I started to smoke marijuana at the end of fifth grade and smoked cigarettes consistently throughout the day. My brother was a big user so I thought it was okay. I became a Rachel that nobody had seen before. I had older friends, and I was using drugs. From then on I was running away, getting into fights, and going to parties. I no longer cared about myself or anybody else.

Things only got worse going into sixth grade. I was addicted to marijuana, and I started to drink alcohol. I let guys take advantage of me, and I used my body to get drugs or sometimes even a place to stay. It seemed like it never mattered anymore to my family where I was. I felt as if I had no family.

My father continued to beat me and my brother until my brother became bigger than him. Then it was them fighting against each other. Sometimes the police weren't even able to break them apart.

The reason why my father hurt and beat us was to hurt my mother. We meant so much to her, but if she screwed up, we would get it worse.

By seventh grade I didn't know where I could start. School was never me. I hated it so I never went. I would not go no matter what. I ran away from school with another friend. We were using drugs and alcohol and sleeping with guys. I got caught under someone's deck and was sent to a foster home. I wasn't at the foster home for long. When I got out, things got worse. I got deeper into drugs. I started going to school because I was court ordered to, but I would not stay the whole day. I failed seventh grade and ended up in summer school.

At this point I was ignoring my dad and not saying hi or anything. I still hated myself and my life. I got sick of being Rachel and going through what I was going through. I tried to kill myself by cutting my wrists. Nothing happened and I wondered why. I knew I didn't deserve more, but why wouldn't I die? I tried many different ways, and that put me through a lot of pain.

I started to be really uneasy, even violent, with everybody that bothered me. All I cared about was drugs. I got into acid and snorting crack at the end of seventh grade summer, and things went downhill. My addiction was worse, and so was my behavior.

My mom saw me cutting on myself and thought I needed help. So she sent me to the hospital. She decided to get her life back on track, so she moved in with my grandma. I played it off like I was better and was not going to get in any more trouble.

When we moved into our own apartment, I had it all. My mom would let me do whatever I wanted and let me have whatever I wanted—clothes, music, friends, everything. But the drugs came jumping into my life again. I felt as if I wasn't a person without them.

When I began eighth grade I was still using. My behaviors were the same and things got worse because I was in charge of the house. I would hurt my mother physically and emotionally to get what I wanted, and hurt myself afterwards for doing so.

I hung around people so old they could be my parents—drug dealers, gang members. I had no education, and I was ill. I didn't eat or sleep for days, even weeks, at a time, because I was using so much, all to cover up how hurt I was. I never got along with my classmates. They thought I was gross, a jerk, and that I never belonged there.

One day at the end of the year, one of the girls who had a life and a home to feel safe in got on my last nerve. She called me a drug dealer and a dopehead, and I lost my temper and beat her up.

One month later I was sent to a treatment center for thirty-six days. When I got out, I still went on with my bad behaviors. I treated my mother like she was nothing, as if she was nobody at all. Three months later I was back in a CD treatment center. I spent almost forty days there. The night I came back I relapsed. My mom was at work that same night, and she never found out. The next day I needed my drugs or my alcohol. What I got or what I had was never enough. So I ran away with a guy who used me for sex and drugs. He disrespected me but made me feel like I deserved it. I was gone for almost one month.

The police came and my boyfriend and his brothers beat up my father. I never cared. I hated him and wanted him to die. I got held in holdover because I was under the influence. I was sent home a couple days later. I made myself believe I wasn't going to change. I beat my mom when I wanted or needed something.

One morning my mom said "no more" and threatened to call the police. I smashed the phones in the house. I took a shower, and, when I got out, the police arrested me for domestic assault. The court ordered me into a treatment facility.

I have been here for three months, wanting and trying to get help and caring about myself and others. I am doing well, but I have work to do yet.

That's my life, and for all of you out there, it's not worth it to be like I was. Stay sober, be safe, and care about yourself, and you'll survive in the BIG WORLD.

# Gangs and Drugs: A Deadly Combination

*Andrew Strockis, age 14*

TWO YEARS AGO WHEN I WAS IN SEVENTH GRADE, I HAD MY FAIR share of problems. I would fight with my parents, participate in gang activities, and sell drugs. I hated life, and I hated myself. It was a never-ending battle between good and evil. I still managed to do well in school, but that was so if I ever pulled out of this life, I would have another.

It all started when a longtime friend moved back into town from Chicago. When he first arrived, he wasted no time establishing his place on the social list. Within months, we were both invited to countless parties and social gatherings. They were all centered around negative things, though. There's no such thing as a free lunch. Soon these friendly parties turned into gang meetings and these gatherings turned into drug deals. At parties, drugs and alcohol were always present and free for use. These were not friendly places during drug deals. Weapons and death threats were not uncommon. At any moment, if somebody called another a liar, all hell would break loose. There would be lots of critically wounded people and sometimes deaths. During deals for pot, only $50 would be spent at one time; deals for more addictive drugs, like crack and coke, might mean several hundred would change hands.

Cops were the enemy and so were other gangs. If any cop was spotted, we would run. We would hop fences and stay off roads and other places where the cops could use cars. Sometimes, friends would be caught; other times we would all escape. I was lucky. Due to my size and resourcefulness, I was never one of the unlucky ones who was caught. If I had been caught, I definitely would have been in trouble for life.

All of this was great for cash. Profits were great and easily spent. Only the real fools used the drugs, smart ones just sold them. I was never one of the ones who sold the stuff, but I was always present. I stayed in the back and made sure nothing would happen to sour the deal. I did my job well and was paid well.

Some people who think their situation is hopeless might think that this is the perfect life. Steady income and plenty of action. Let me tell you, it is hell on earth. Nothing is worse than wondering what will happen today and praying that you aren't caught (or worse). It is terrible to suddenly realize that your friends and life are all trash. As you look around, all you see is crime and corruption. Death looms over you like a shadow that never disappears. It is like living a terrible nightmare. Reach down into the deepest bowels of your heart and imagine the worst possible nightmare that you could have, and that won't even come close. For all of you who consider this a life, don't make the same mistake I did. Don't do it. Trust me, no matter how terrible life seems now, it can get five times worse.

Since then I have shaped up. I no longer live my life to the book of corruption. I have made new friends and abolished my old practices. I now live a normal life, and, while not perfect, I am much better off. I was lucky. Others are crack fiends, and still others continue what they are doing until prison or death stops them. Be smart and learn from my mistakes. You might not be as lucky as I was; you might be stuck for life.

# Struggle

*Matthew, age 17*

THROUGHOUT MY LIFE, I HAVE FACED MANY HARDSHIPS, BUT NONE as hard as getting out of the drug world. I entered it in the summer of my eighth grade year, out of a combination of curiosity and too much time on my hands. All my friends were smoking marijuana, and I needed their love and acceptance. At first I told them that they were dumb for smoking it. I thought I would never stoop to their level of stupidity! Within a few months I was passing the joint with the rest of them.

I did not think I had a problem. I was starting defensive back on the freshman football team, I was keeping my grades up, and I was dating a junior. Besides, my parents did not have a clue. I felt like everything was going my way. What I did not realize, at the time, was that for every action there is a consequence, and my actions were building up consequences I could never have foreseen.

I first realized I had a problem when my girlfriend dumped me. I thought I didn't care, and I told myself I just used her like she used me. I did not shed a tear. I did, however, increase the amount of drugs flowing into my body. One of my favorite combinations was alcohol and marijuana. I felt like I was doing somersaults and forgetting all my problems at the same time—what a deal! I later learned from my father, who is a doctor, that I could have died very easily from alcohol poisoning this way.

Because I never dealt with my loss, it ate away at my insides. I became angry. Then, during the start of my sophomore year, I began going to church. Church was something I had been avoiding for quite awhile; maybe I was avoiding God. I realized I was sinning and stopped everything. I was determined to live a Christian life.

I never was truly happy in my new environment. I felt like I had thrown away all my good times, and I missed my friends. I became depressed. My bitterness and hurt fed my anger. Then one of my friends came back from a rehabilitation clinic and was invited to my church. He wasn't happy either. After three months of sobriety, we both got sucked back in.

It was just on the weekends at first, but I began to partake of the herb's magical powers more and more frequently. So began my downward slide into the mire. As my black hole of need grew larger, I filled it with more and more. LSD, cocaine, crack, pills, and inhalants all became a part of my life. I started dealing drugs to support my habit. To me, marijuana was no longer something to look forward to. It was something I used morning, noon, and night just to feel "normal."

By my junior year my grades began to drop, and I lost interest in everything around me. I lost interest in living. My life had become tasteless, colorless, meaningless. Suicidal thoughts were not uncommon, and my attitude reflected it.

At about this time, my parents wised up and realized something was wrong. Around Christmastime they admitted me into a rehab program as an outpatient. They still did not realize the seriousness of my problem, so I continued to smoke daily behind their backs, even though I took drug tests every Friday. Amazingly, they thought I had quit; they had never been further from the truth.

But eventually, as all deception does, it came to light. My parents took away everything that could be considered a freedom and let me rot in my house. I had a fairly large stash of drugs, so I used them until they ran out. Also, my dealer lived near my home, and he would smoke with me almost every night. I could have continued the fight, but something inside me softened, and I stayed sober for a couple of weeks. That was the beginning of the end for me, although it took a day-by-day struggle and God's grace to pull me through.

I am now approaching my one-year anniversary of sobriety. My life has never changed so much in such a short time. I started going back to church, and the people there lifted me up when I had no strength. Now I am in a position to help others, because I am part of the mid-school ministry. I help to write the lessons and lead the sixth grade boys' prayer group. If God Himself had appeared to me and told me I would be here today, I would have laughed at the inconceivability of it.

The whole reason I have written this is to encourage anyone who might be going through the same struggle. Maybe I am writing this to someone who is not struggling at all, who cannot imagine life any other way. God knows there are millions of you, and He wants to help you. Supporting friends who offer encouragement are a tremendous help, but believing in yourself and wanting to change are essential. Set your mind to it, and get things right with God. He can break off your chains—He can set you free. I know, because He has done it for me.

# Don't Be Afraid to Say No

*Kimberly Agnew, age 14*

I AM A FOURTEEN-YEAR-OLD TEENAGE GIRL WITH A LOT OF PROB-lems, a bad attitude, and a drug problem. I guess that you're wondering what kind of problems, why a bad attitude, and whether I still have a drug problem. Well, I'm going to tell you. I have the same problems that a regular teenager has, plus I am on probation. I have a very bad temper, and I like guyfriends more than girlfriends. My bad attitude is from the drugs. I like being in charge, and I don't like not getting what I want. I do, and always will, have a drug problem. I have been in a drug abuse program and I have learned how to say no to drugs, but I will always have problems.

Other people who know me think that I am a sweet, loveable, respectable, understanding, and innocent person. I disagree; I don't see myself like that. A lot of people have told me that I am a beautiful and great person. Sometimes I disagree. Sometimes I think that I am neither beautiful nor great.

I have gotten to where I am today by listening to what people have to say, especially my drug abuse class and my family. I have had many people who were always there for me. My friends stood by my side. My family was there for me, except for my dad. My probation officer listened to me, and my drug abuse counselor was always there for me.

I wrote the following letter to show you that I am not afraid to say no. It's not easy to say no to drugs. It's not easy to quit doing them. One thing to remember is that in the end, they only hurt you and the people you love.

*Dear Drugs,*

*I'm writing to tell you that you were like my best friend. You were always there when I needed you. Sometimes, I wish you were still there, especially in situations like one Friday night when the guy that helps run the drug abuse class got a wild hair up his butt and said, "The only thing you do best is screw," or when some kids in school say, "The only reason you are going out with a twenty-two-year-old is because he pays you for having sex with him." I sometimes wish that I wasn't on probation so I could use when I am in a using mood. I have needed you to take my pain away, and, at one time, I thanked you.*

*I realized tonight that I don't need you to make me happy. I don't need you to have fun. I want you out of my life, because you did nothing but hurt me more than I was already hurting. I also realized tonight that I have lost and done a lot of things because of you. I lost a little memory. I lost respect for myself. I lost respect from my family and people I cared about. I did things I wouldn't have done if you hadn't been there.*

*I am stopping you because you have done nothing but mess up my life. You are the one who got me in bad spots. You made me sick and caused me to hate the people I loved and cared about. You aren't what I need. What I need is to find out who I am. I have to start respecting myself before I get involved with a man. I just wanted to tell you that you were like a best friend, but now you're not. I am asking you not to come around me anymore. I don't need you or want you, because I am trying to change my life for good, not bad.*

*I wish you were gone, but you never will be, because I will always have my memories.*

*Your Ex-User*

I would like to give all teenagers some advice. You need to listen to what I have to say. If you are doing drugs, get some help. Don't let your friends pressure you into doing drugs. If they do, they're not your true friends. You need to respect your parents. You need to listen to what people have to say. You need to be open-minded about what people say.

I would like to thank everyone who has taken the time to read my story. I would like to thank everyone who has ever helped me. I hope that whoever reads this story learns something from it. I wish everyone good luck.

# ILLNESS AND DISABILITY

# Champion of Life

........................................................

*Joshua Sundquist, age 13*

MOST TEN-YEAR-OLDS ARE BUSY. BUSY WITH THEIR FRIENDS. BUSY playing outside. Busy with sports or other activities. Some are busy getting their hair to look nice.

But I wasn't like most ten-year-olds. While my friends were counting the score at their baseball games, I was counting my days in the hospital. While they were playing, I was too tired to get out of bed. While they were getting a new haircut, I couldn't. I didn't have any hair. I had cancer.

I started having pains in my left leg when I was eight years old. They became very intense, so I went to the doctor. After several different medical tests, I was diagnosed with a rare form of bone cancer. Having your parents tell you that you have cancer in your left leg is quite a scare. I thought this meant that I was going to die, but they explained that chemotherapy and surgery can get rid of cancer.

I immediately began chemotherapy treatment. Chemotherapy, or chemo, for short, is a special kind of medicine designed to kill fast-growing cells, such as cancer. Hair is also made of fast-growing cells. This is why most people lose their hair when they start chemo. When my hair started to fall out, my friends decided to show their support—about twenty of them came over to my house to have their heads shaved!

After three chemo treatments, the size of the tumor had not changed. Because it covered such a large area, my family and I had to decide if I should have my leg amputated. After much thought and prayer, we agreed that amputation seemed the best option. On July 6,

1994, my leg was amputated from the hip. Because this was such a major surgery, the doctors expected me to stay in the hospital for three weeks. I recovered so quickly, however, that they sent me home after just five days! But even though the surgery was successful and I healed quickly, I had to continue chemo for another nine months.

In the course of a year, I had eighteen chemo treatments. Each of these required a three- to five-day stay in the hospital. The children's medical center where I was treated offered games, a computer, a TV show, and other fun activities, but I was so tired that I stayed in bed most of the time. Normally, I had two weeks between chemotherapy cycles. I always felt bad during the first week—I was tired and I didn't feel like eating. Just when I was starting to feel a little better, it was time to return to the hospital.

Soon after my amputation, I was fitted with an artificial leg, which attaches around my waist. It has a hip joint that bends when I sit down, and a knee joint that bends so I can walk normally. Until I got my artificial leg, I had been using crutches to get around. After getting my leg, I started physical therapy so I could learn how to use it. It took only five days for me to complete my therapy and walk without assistance.

The only way to deal with cancer is to take life one day at a time. Looking ahead to a year of chemotherapy can be a bit overwhelming. Each morning you wake up, you have to tell yourself, "I can make it through this day." I focused on that goal. I never took my eyes off the time when I would finish treatment. Life without goals is like a race without a finish line. Without a finish line, there is no reason to carry on. I also kept my eyes on God. If God wasn't holding my hand through the storm, the winds would have knocked me over. It is by His grace that I stand today.

I did finish. In the spring of 1995, I finished my last chemo treatment. Slowly, my hair grew back. My appetite returned, and now I am always hungry. I am still missing a leg, of course, but it doesn't hold me back.

Several months after I finished treatment, I learned to ride a bike. Biking on and off road is now one of my favorite activities. A year ago I completed a fifty-mile bike ride. I also ski a lot and have won medals in several disabled competitions. Swimming, volleyball, soccer, playing drums, and jumping on my backyard trampoline are some other activities I enjoy.

I often speak to groups about getting through tough times. Through my loss, I can help them gain an appreciation for life. I have been on the national Children's Miracle Network (CMN) telethon to raise money for children's hospitals. I have been on the local CMN broadcast several times as well. Last February, I spoke at the International RE/MAX Realtors convention in Nashville, Tennessee. There were five thousand people there!

Today, I am a busy thirteen-year-old. I am busy playing sports and doing things with friends, and I try to keep my hair looking nice. I am living proof that you can overcome life's challenges. When hard times come to you, you must make a choice. Either you will persist and overcome, or you will run and hide. In hiding, your life will only waste away. But if you take risks and have courage, you will become a true champion of life.

# All for Mother

*Anonymous, age 17*

I'D BEEN HEARING HER ALARM FOR TOO LONG. IT WAS THE KIND that didn't shut off until the button was pressed. It had been buzzing and beeping for fifteen minutes straight. I couldn't believe she could sleep through it.

I went to the doorway to her room. "Mom?" I called. There was no answer.

"Mom!"

I cracked the door. She was snoring. She was louder than I thought a person could be when they were asleep.

"Mom!"

I tapped her. I pushed her. I shook her. I couldn't wake her. Her snoring only got louder, and then I realized that it wasn't snoring at all. She was making a flapping noise with her lips and snorting through her nose.

Something was wrong.

I ran to wake my sister. Together we called 911. The sheriff and the firefighters and the ambulance people were at our door within minutes. They began to ask me questions.

"Has she ever had a seizure before?"

"A seizure? No. That's what this is?"

I remembered, only then, what everyone had explained to me nine months earlier. After my mother had had her brain surgery in the fall, there was always the possibility that she could have a seizure. I never thought it would really happen, though. And it hadn't, until now.

They put her in the ambulance and took her away. My sister and I sat on the couch, silently. We waited for someone to come tell us what to do, but we were alone. Finally my sister said: "Weren't you supposed to take your SAT this morning?"

I had almost forgotten. "Yeah," I said. "But . . . I can take it next time."

"Next year?"

It was June. "Huhh? Oh, yeah. I'll take it next year."

She looked at me. "I think you should take it now."

"But, Mommy's sick, and—"

"Jenna. She'll feel bad if she makes you miss it."

"I know, but—"

"Jenna."

"Fine, okay. Whatever. But I'm going to do really bad, Karen. Watch."

***

I had been stressed about the SAT for weeks. I already felt like a fool for waiting until the end of my junior year to take it. If I blew it, there would be so few chances to take it again.

But with my mother in the hospital, my fear vanished. I'd heard once that the human body can only feel one kind of pain at a time. I decided that the same was true for fear. I was afraid for my mother's safety, her survival. The test meant nothing in comparison to that.

My aunt and sister drove me to the testing site; my dad would pick me up. I'd been late to register for the SAT, so I'd been assigned to a school about an hour from my house. I didn't know where it was; my mother had known the way. I was sure I wouldn't make it. I didn't want to make it. I wanted to turn around and go back to my mother.

Amazingly, five minutes before the test began, we found it. It caught me off-guard; I'd been ready to go back home. But I got out of the car like I was supposed to, I walked up to the school like I was supposed to, and I sat down and took my test because I was supposed to.

Before I opened the test, I reminded myself that my future was not riding on this. I was doing it for my mother. If I didn't take it, she would feel bad. It didn't matter what I got. I would take it in the fall and it would matter then.

I found it surprisingly easy to concentrate. I did not seem to be thinking about anything. The answers formed in the empty space that was my mind. When I got distracted, when I stared at the chalkboard and wondered if my mother would live, I caught myself and refocused.

Between each section of the test, I closed my eyes and prayed. I'm sure I wasn't the only one in the school sending out prayers that morning. But my prayers were not SAT-related.

My family was an hour late coming to get me. I had hoped they'd be longer. It had occurred to me that as long as I was sitting cross-legged on the lawn of the high school, I was still a girl with a mother. As soon as the burgundy Chevy pulled into the parking lot and I stood up and saw my dad's or sister's face, I would know whether or not my mother was dead.

I held my breath the moment I saw the car turn down the street. Only when it was in front of me did I dare to look up. I caught my sister's eye. She was smiling. I exhaled slowly. I was so relieved, it hurt.

\*\*\*

My mother sat straight up in the hospital bed when she saw me.

"Are you okay?" I asked tentatively.

"I'm fine. Are you okay?"

I laughed lightly. "Of course."

She looked at me. I saw that she was nearly in tears. "I'm so sorry."

I hugged her. "Mom. For what? Everything's okay."

"Did you do okay?"

"It doesn't matter. I can take it five times next year."

"Was it hard?"

I paused. "I can't remember." And I really couldn't.

* * *

I'd been told I'd get my scores within a month. They came in two weeks. My sister sat with me while I studied the envelope.

"Are you going to open it?"

"Wait," I said. I swung the envelope between my thumb and forefinger. As long as the envelope was closed, I might still be a girl with a future.

She snatched it. "Do you want me to do it?"

I took it back. "No. Here I go." I opened my future.

The first score to jump at me was a 570. Then I saw a 710.

"Karen!" I screamed. "I got a 1260!"

She took the letter. "No wonder you scored higher in English. That's a 1280."

"A what?" I could hardly breathe. I had barely touched 1050 in my practice tests.

"A 1280." She shook her head slowly. "Wait until the colleges get a look at this."

"No," I said. I took the letter back. "Wait until Mom gets a look at this."

# Living with Spina Bifida

......................................................

*Anonymous, age 14*

FOURTEEN YEARS AGO I WAS BORN WITH A BIRTH DEFECT CALLED spina bifida. Spina bifida is the most frequently occurring permanently disabling birth defect. It affects approximately one out of every 1,000 newborns in the United States. More children have spina bifida than have muscular dystrophy and cystic fibrosis combined. Spina bifida, the most common neural tube defect, is one of the most devastating of all birth defects. It results from the failure of the spine to close properly during the first month of pregnancy. In severe cases, the spinal cord comes through the back and may be covered by skin or a thin membrane. Surgery to close a newborn's back is generally performed within twenty-four hours after birth to minimize the risk of infection and to preserve existing function in the spinal cord. I had that done when I was one day old.

Because of the paralysis resulting from the damage to the spinal cord, people born with spina bifida may need surgeries and other extensive medical care. The condition can also cause bowel and bladder complications. A large percentage of children born with spina bifida also have hydrocephalus, the accumulation of fluid in the brain. Hydrocephalus is controlled by a surgical procedure called "shunting" which relieves the fluid buildup in the brain by redirecting it into the abdominal area.

I have most of the complications of spina bifida, but I am also luckier than most of the children born with spina bifida. I am able to walk without any support or the use of a wheelchair.

This past year has not been a good year for me. I have had six major surgeries in the last eight months. It has been very hard on our entire family because they worry so much about me. I tell them that we should be thankful for what we have. Spending so much time at a children's hospital has shown me that all of my problems are small in comparison to what other children are going through. We have learned to enjoy each good day, and we try not worry about what tomorrow may bring. Life is a gift which we should all treasure.

I have been out of school since last September, so I have had a teacher come to my home to help me keep up with my studies. Doing well in school is very important to me.

My dream for the future is to become a nurse and work at a children's hospital. I want to give children everything that has been given to me—caring, hope, and compassion.

# Just the Basics: My Father's Story

*A.M. Wells, age 14*

MY FATHER'S STORY BEGAN IN AUGUST OF 1960, ON HIS FATHER'S forty-seventh birthday—the day his father had a sudden heart attack and died. Since then, my father and his two brothers had been in good health, and they did not seem to be in danger.

One morning many years later, my father woke up early—very early—for no apparent reason. He was anxious and sweaty and had some indigestion. He thought nothing of it, however, because he was about to go through a job change and had eaten bratwurst not long before at a Memorial Day celebration. He decided to take a walk, thinking he just needed to relax. But after walking for a while, he was still not calming down. Living not too far from the hospital, he decided to go see if the doctor could give him some medicine to calm him.

In the emergency room, the nurse took my father's blood pressure. Although the numbers looked a little odd, they soon straightened out. Just to be cautious, they did an EKG (electrocardiogram). A doctor told my father he believed he had just had a heart attack. They immediately put him on morphine and oxygen and drew his blood to check for heart enzymes, which are only present in the blood when heart muscle damage has taken place. Oddly enough, there were no heart enzymes in my father's blood, but the doctors were very sure that he had, in fact, had a heart attack. He was hospitalized for about three weeks total (he was discharged once but had to go back).

My father had been home from the hospital for several weeks, recuperating, when my mother went into labor with their second child (me). She was taken to the same hospital that my father had been admitted to when he had his heart attack. Doctors advised my father that he could watch the birth as long as he wore a heart monitor so they could keep an eye on him. At one point, the cardiology staff monitoring his heart called down to the delivery room and said that my father had to go out to the waiting room for a bit because his heart had skipped a few beats, but he was able to come back for the actual birth.

After my father's heart attack, everything seemed fine. Then, in 1993, ten years later, one of his brothers died of a sudden heart attack at the age of forty-six. This hit my father hard because his brother died at about the same age as their father, and he himself was heading toward his mid-forties.

On Friday, September 22, 1995, a little over thirteen years from his first heart attack, my father experienced his second. The doctors did not see it as too serious. He was scheduled to go to some specialists in ten days and maybe get on a transplant list for a future transplant. They did not think that an immediate transplant was necessary, so he was hospitalized for a week and discharged on Friday, September 29, his youngest daughter's seventh birthday.

When our family sat down to birthday dinner, my father was not feeling well enough to join us at the kitchen table, so my mother brought him some food in the living room, thinking he was still kind of weak from the heavy medications. He didn't even feel well enough to eat. Soon he started to sweat a lot and have several other symptoms that he had experienced during his second heart attack, and he began to call for help. My mother was in the living room while the rest of us were in the kitchen, watching from across the room as my father begged for someone to call 911. As soon as my mother realized what was happening she called. They said they were sending a response team but let my mother hang up so she could call his cardiologist. My mother tried to call the doctor at home at the number on my father's discharge papers, but this was the wrong phone number. She tried to call the doctor's office to get the correct home phone number, but the receptionist refused to give it to her, saying that she wasn't allowed to. My mother tried to explain to her that my father was having another heart attack and she needed to speak to the doctor immediately, but the receptionist held out. Finally my mother hung up the phone, exasperated, and tried to help my father, who had begun to have trouble breathing.

My father was rushed to the hospital in an ambulance. He was put on a heart bypass machine to try to keep him alive until more help came. His heart stopped several times that night, and it was hard to tell if he would make it. He needed immediate help, and the doctors felt the best thing to do would be to send him to a hospital with an artificial heart. At this time, out of the six hospitals in the country with artificial heart technology, LDS Hospital in Salt Lake City, Utah, was the only one that would take my father. They sent some specialists up in a Life Flight helicopter and rushed him to Salt Lake City.

My father was on the artificial heart for seventy-two days. He had to push around a large console-type computer everywhere he went, but it kept him alive until a donor heart was located. His own heart, which had experienced so much damage it took up 80 percent of his chest cavity, had been removed before the artificial one was placed. It was just a matter of time and patience.

On December 11, 1995, my father got the news that a forty-five-year-old Salt Lake City man had had a brain aneurysm and had died not long after being taken to LDS. His heart was a perfect match with my father's and was the first one made available to him. He received the transplant that day and began his recovery.

My father had to begin taking anti-rejection medicines, which suppressed his immune system, as well as many, many other types of medications to keep something from going wrong. He will have to take these for the rest of his life, but their dosages will decrease.

My father was discharged from the hospital on December 22. The hospital had recently purchased a little house within walking distance that was supposed to be used for people on an L-VAD (Left Ventricular Assist Device), which is like a partial artificial heart. So the house was called "the L-VAD house." My father was allowed to stay there, however, since he had just had a transplant and needed to be close to the hospital so they could monitor his progress. He was the first to stay in this house.

The night of December 22, right after my father took his things over to the L-VAD house, he was loaded into a hospital van in a wheelchair and a Santa hat, with a surgical face mask to keep him from getting an infection, and taken to the Salt Lake City airport to meet his family. We were expecting to be met by a family friend who was to take us to my father's temporary house, but when we walked through the doors, my dad took off his face mask and stood up from the wheelchair. We were overjoyed. We spent Christmas together in that L-VAD house as a family, sometimes not saying anything at all, just happy to be together. The night that we left was the first night since September that my father had spent alone, without machines, without nurses, without family. It was very hard for him.

On April 7, 1996, my father was allowed to come home to South Dakota. He frequently goes back to LDS in Salt Lake City for biopsies, laboratory tests, echocardiograms, and such to make sure that he is still in good health and his body is not rejecting his heart. He has had no complications since and is more active than ever with his new heart.

# Mother

*LaShondra Webster, age 16*

*Leaving me is something I'll hate*
*Although the pain I'll have to take*
*Usually holding my feelings inside*
*Realizing it's something I just can't hide*
*As for now you're here right by my side*
*Whether you're happy or sad*
*Living life good or bad*
*Not doing wrong but right*
*Your life can change*
*From darkness to light*

I'VE OVERCOME MANY OBSTACLES IN LIFE BUT, SO FAR, ONLY ONE has been so meaningful that it continues to affect me.

Last year, my mother became very sick. Not knowing what was wrong, she went to the hospital for a checkup. When she returned home, she told us that the doctors had an idea of what was wrong, but that they would need to run more tests to be certain.

The doctors soon diagnosed my mother with cancer. The instant she informed me, I felt as if my heart had stopped. All the thoughts in my head were blank, my life was at a standstill. I had no previous knowledge of cancer, and the little I did know led me to the conclusion that my mother was going to die. My mother, however, had no doubts about her well-being; she simply told me to be strong and to pray.

After many visits to the hospital and lots of information classes, my mother chose chemotherapy as her form of treatment.

I watched as my mother grew weaker and weaker. Though there were many times when I wanted to cry, I didn't. I felt like I was being strong for both of us. I thought that if I broke down, she would soon follow.

I watched as this strong black woman—mother of seven, lover of life, a woman who had been through things most people have never dreamed of—turn helpless and almost childlike.

The role of mother and daughter had been switched. I found myself taking care of her. It was like a sign from God, telling me that my mother was not going to be able to take care of me the rest of my life and that, at some point, I'd have to do things on my own.

The chemotherapy was working, and she was recovering quickly. After about eight months, my mother was becoming her old self again.

Though painful, I feel that this ordeal has helped me a lot. I realized that anything can happen to you or your loved ones, and in the blink of an eye your whole life can change, whether for better or worse. We all know where we've been, but no one knows where they're going. I live life for today, because who knows what tomorrow has in store.

# My Brother

*Valerie , age 13*

HELLO, MY NAME IS VALERIE, AND I HAVE A STORY TO TELL. YOU see, this story is about my brother, who is disabled. I want to share this experience with everyone, because most people think that people with disabilities are dumb and can't do anything.

It all started when my brother and parents went to visit my grandparents in Mexico. My brother was about two-and-a-half years old. He got very sick. My mom thought it was a normal sickness. Over the next few days, my brother developed a high fever. My mom began to worry, so she and my father took my brother to a doctor.

The doctor checked my brother and came to the conclusion that he simply had a high fever and there was nothing to worry about. My parents believed him, since he was a doctor.

When my parents and brother returned home, my brother stopped talking. All he did was mumble. Before he got sick, he was able to say words like "mama," "papa," "food," and "bano." It got to the point where all he could say was "mmm."

My mom and my dad got divorced. When my younger sister was born, my mom had to do everything on her own, like taking care of me and my sister and still take care of my brother. He had to be treated like a baby because he couldn't do anything on his own.

My brother went to so many doctors, but the worst thing about it was that they didn't know what he had, which was mental retardation.

As I got older and saw that my brother was sick, I started to feel ashamed of him. Everyone made fun of him and called him names like "retard," "idiot," and "moron." When I saw what people were saying about him, I used to call him the same things, maybe worse.

The one thing I hated was when I couldn't go outside without taking my brother with me. I used to feel embarrassed to be out with him.

My mom would tell me that I had to be nice to my brother instead of talking about him all the time. I remember when my brother used to make a mess and then I would get blamed for it. I would tell my mom that it was my brother and not me, but my mom would say that my brother was not capable of making such a mess. So my mom wouldn't believe me, and that used to get me into trouble and make me so mad because I was always cleaning up his mess.

Once my parents were divorced, it seemed as if I was the one doing all the work, but it really wasn't me who was doing all the work, it was my mother. Sometimes, I would try to help my mom as much as I could because she would go to sleep exhausted from having to do so much, besides having to go to work.

I was gradually beginning to accept the fact that my brother was disabled and that there was a possibility he wouldn't get better. I was still ashamed, but all I really wanted was for my brother to get better.

My mom finally found the right doctor for my brother. The doctor said that my brother had had a high fever, and since it hadn't been treated right away, it had affected his brain, the part of the brain that controls speech, and that was why he couldn't talk. The doctor also said my mom could have sued the doctor who took care of my brother. My mom had waited too long, so it was too late to sue him.

Well, when I was in fifth grade, my grudge over having a disabled brother finally wore off. I guess I had matured and could better understand the condition that my brother was in. Since then, my brother and I have developed a loving relationship. I try to look beyond his disability and toward his good qualities. I do not regret having a disabled brother, because I've learned that God does things for a reason and we should just let everything be.

# Keeping Hope Alive

......................................................

*Elvira Rodriguez, age 18*

I CAN REMEMBER A COUPLE OF YEARS AGO WHEN I WAS SWITCHING channels on TV, trying to find something to watch, and I came across this news report about breast cancer. I didn't know much about it at the time and didn't really care because I thought, "Hey it doesn't affect me," so I changed the channel.

Times have changed since then. Whenever I hear the words "breast cancer," I pay attention. I want to learn everything I possibly can about the disease since I am at risk of getting it when I'm older. My whole thinking about breast cancer changed when I learned my mother was a victim of this fatal epidemic that many women face today.

About two years ago I remember coming home from the movies with my brother. When we walked through the door my mother had this somber look on her face and I knew something was wrong. She told me she had felt this lump on her breast. To be on the safe side she went to see the doctor about it. The doctor scheduled her for some mammograms to detect what the lump was. He told her it could possibly be breast cancer.

The day my mother was diagnosed with breast cancer will forever be imprinted in my memory. I remember being in the hospital room with my mom and two brothers when the doctor walked in with the results of the mammograms. I saw the look on his face and knew it wasn't good news. He confirmed our worst fears—my mother had breast cancer. I felt like someone had punched me in the stomach. I had a pain in my heart I had never felt before. I cried and cried, tears streaming down my face and the whole time I thought, "How can this be happening?"

My mother's life, as well as my brothers' and my life, changed after that day. My mother had surgery to remove the lump before it spread. After that she was forced to go through chemotherapy. Chemo was probably the hardest thing my mother had to go through. She lost all her hair, which was a very emotional thing for her. She was also very ill after each chemo treatment she received. Many times she cried and confided in me that she didn't know if she could take another chemo treatment. She hated the way she felt and looked. But for six months she took the pain, emotionally and physically.

Later, my mother was able to have reconstructive breast surgery. Times were hard during those months with my mother in and out of the hospital, so I helped any way I could, both around the house and taking care of her when she was sick. Our friends and family helped make it bearable with all their prayers and support. They even held a barbecue benefit to raise money to help my mom pay the bills, since she missed work a lot. It was nice to know people cared.

It's been three years since my mom was diagnosed with breast cancer, and she looks good. She's healthy and back to her old self again. Since my mother had breast cancer, I know I am at high risk of getting it. I have to take care of myself.

I fear that if I do get breast cancer, I won't be strong enough to take it like my mom. I saw everything she had to go through and I think, "I can't go through what she did." But then I think, my mother didn't give up, she didn't let her fears get the best of her. She kept her head up, never giving up hope. I know that whatever God has dealt for me in life I have to take it, whether it be breast cancer or something else. I can never give up hope, because my mother never did.

# My Story

...................................................

*Kiersten Johnson, age 16*

WHEN MRS. JOHNSON TAKES HER COUGHING, WHEEZING, FOUR-year-old daughter to the doctor's office, she expects the worst: bronchitis. The doctor inspects the little girl and announces that the cough is just a bad case of asthma. He sends her home with some medication and asks to see her again in a week.

At the end of the week, Kiersten's breathing and coughing have gotten worse. Worried and confused, Mrs. Johnson takes the child back to the doctor, who refers her to a throat and lung specialist at Stanford Hospital. At Stanford, Dr. Blessing (yes, this is his real name—isn't that ironic?) discovers that Kiersten is not suffering from asthma. The problem is coming from the throat and neck area; asthma comes from the chest and lungs.

After a number of tests, the doctors come to a horrible conclusion: Kiersten has a malignant case of Medullary Thyroid Carcinoma, a fatal type of cancer. The little girl, scared and bewildered by what is happening to her tiny body, is immediately sent to be operated on. Kiersten's family, trying to explain what is happening without scaring her, tell her that the Big Bad Wolf is after her. This is what they call her disease whenever she is present.

The operation takes a total of eight-and-a-half hours. The surgeons discover that part of the tumor is tangled around Kiersten's vocal chords. Knowing that they can't possibly retrieve it without causing even more damage, they decide to try an alternative treatment to save her. Since chemotherapy does not have a positive effect on this type of cancer, doctors are forced to send Kiersten to radiation.

For the next two months, Kiersten undergoes radiation treatment five times a week. She loses all the soft, blonde hair at the back of her head and becomes frail and weak from the killer medicine. Kiersten is up to the last ounce of radiation she can handle before it kills her when, finally, the treatment works. Her thankful family is glad to have the nightmare over. But it isn't over. They still have a ways to go.

In time, Kiersten's hair grows out and she starts school. Everyone lives in peace for three years, until Kiersten, now seven years old, goes in for her annual MRI to check for cancer cells. Tragically, the cancer has returned to its nesting spot in the girl's thyroid gland. Doctors and family members are stumped and confused. How could she possibly survive this deadly cancer again? She can't handle any more radiation, and this is what saved her the last time. The only thing they can do is operate.

Family and friends are frightened; they couldn't bare to lose the only girl in the family. She is such a joy; how could such a terrible thing happen to her? They try to stay hopeful.

Luckily, the doctors find the tumor just in the nick of time. The cancer has not spread. They retrieve the cancer by taking out her thyroid gland, and Kiersten and her family enjoy seven more years of happiness before facing yet another challenge.

During a regular physical-education screening in middle school, Kiersten's teacher realizes that she has scoliosis—a virus of the spine that causes it to twist and turn. Doctors prescribe a back brace for Kiersten to wear every night for at least ten hours. Made of hard plastic, the odd-looking contraption is designed to hold the body in the opposite direction of the curve—a backward "S" shape. Although Kiersten detests this "torture chamber," she wears the brace each night, often crying herself to sleep. After a year, however, the doctors decide that there is no way to avoid the treacherous, five-hour surgery to correct Kiersten's back. The operation is scheduled for March 20, 1997.

Kiersten's family drives to Lake Tahoe for Christmas, but they cut their trip short when Kiersten passes out from the thin air and high altitude. Something must be terribly wrong for this to happen. Mrs. Johnson takes Kiersten to her pediatrician right away. Within a week, she is referred to a lung specialist, Dr. Conrad, who starts a series of tests to locate the problem. The weeks go by, and the day of Kiersten's back surgery draws near. About three weeks before the big day, Dr. Conrad finds some suspicious-looking spots in Kiersten's lungs. To determine what these spots are, a biopsy is scheduled in place of the back operation.

Unfortunately, the results are positive. Cancer has been slowly taking over Kiersten's body for the sixteen years of her life. It has spread to her lungs. Because of the late detection, there is nothing the doctors can do to save her life. Although Kiersten's future looks grim, everyone tries to keep a positive attitude. They are trying all sorts of holistic approaches, including vitamin supplements to boost her immune system, in the hope of avoiding what must happen to us all. Death.

***

Dear Reader,

Hi, it's me again. Kiersten. This isn't part of my essay, just a little note of personal advice I would like to pass on. Live your life to the fullest! Try not to get so caught up with today's society—with appointments, schedules, and what other people think of you. Be yourself! Take a moment to look around at this wonderful world! Take time to visit the people you mean to visit "one day," because you never know when you will be one day too late. I never really did these things before I was rediagnosed. Yes, I've always loved living and everything about it, but I didn't appreciate it half as much as I do now. It saddens me to see people so stressed out over the tiny details of life. Okay, well, I must say 'bye for now. I hope that you enjoyed reading "My Story" as much as I enjoyed writing it.

# RACISM

# Wrong Sex, Wrong Color

*Rayvon Scott, age 16*

I AM NOT AN EXPERT ON IGNORANCE, NOR DO I HAVE A DEGREE IN race relations. I cannot read deep within the confused minds of racist people and try to sympathize, nor do I have a desire to do so.

So what do I desire? I long to see the day when all people can understand how it feels when we discriminate and commit racist crimes against one another. Most of all, I wish for people to see that black and white aren't the only colors in the rainbow, and that not all things that are different are wrong. It is my sincere wish that with this story, I will help create a glimmer of hope in a dim and confused world.

During the time that I lived in Philadelphia, I was reckless. Wherever I was, trouble was my constant companion. So my long-time friend and Bible Club teacher, Ms. Christine, decided to find me a mentor. I guess she thought I needed a positive male role model, and as hard as it may seem, she found me one. His name is Larry, and if it were not for the purpose of this story, I wouldn't even remember that I am black and he is white.

At 8:30 in the morning, I was dressed, packed, and ready to go. I turned on the news for the weather. The insta-racist forecast called for prejudice with a slight chance of harassment. Larry had called the night before to ask if I could baby-sit his two children, five-year-old Shelby and three-year-old Brendon. I said sure. I asked my best friend Pete to come along so we could work together. I began to look for my umbrella, but they had not created a shield against the racist downpour I was about to endure.

The children were happy to see us. They began to shout "Rayvon, Rayvon, can you play with us?" I said sure, and we played games until it was time for lunch. After lunch, Larry's wife, Heather, asked if we could take the children to the park down the street, so we suited them up, put them in a wagon, and began our journey.

As we walked, Pete turned to me and said, "Hey, Ray, wouldn't it be funny if someone saw us struggling down the street with them two and thought we were trying to kidnap them?" I laughed and said, "Yeah. We're some great felons, kidnapping two white kids in the middle of a predominately white neighborhood, using a wagon as our getaway car. Brilliant."

We spoke to some of their neighbors as we passed by, and soon we had reached our destination: the playground.

Things were going good for a while, until we saw the lights. I was sitting on the jungle gym, tired, out of breath, just beginning to realize that my own energy was no match for the two Energizer Bunnies, when a police officer walked up. He spoke to Pete first, then signaled for me to join them. He began to ask a series of tiring and utterly belittling questions, such as "Why are you here?" and "How did you get here?" He then proceeded to ask what I thought was the most idiotic question of the evening, "Do you know these children?" even as the children pulled on our legs, saying, "Rayvon, Pete, come play with us!"

After the officer finished his interrogation, I asked, "What seems to be the problem?" I realize that this is not the proper way to address the law, but at that moment, I was upset. The officer said they had received a call from a "concerned citizen" about some "suspicious characters lurking around the neighborhood." He said he was sorry for the inconvenience and that we would be hearing from him soon.

Afterward, Pete and I felt like laughing and crying at the same time. We had been violated and disrespected, but we didn't let that stop the children from having fun. When we gathered up everyone to make our way home, we felt like we really had committed a crime.

When we arrived home, we told Larry and Heather about the sickening event that had occurred. They became very upset. Larry called the police department, filed a complaint against the officer, and asked for the name of the person who had called in such an "obnoxious and blatantly ignorant complaint." He talked to a congressman, who was a good friend of his, and published an article in the city newspaper.

Eventually, a town meeting was held to discuss the contents of the Neighborhood Watchers' handbook, which stated that they should report any "suspicious" activity to the police. The community is still buzzing over the meaning of the word "suspicious."

What will come of all this? I'm not sure. I learned that ignorance can take any shape or form. It can try to destroy you, but that doesn't mean you have to succumb to it.

Later, after the controversy had calmed down, I was asked how I felt about all the trials and tribulations we had been through. I had this to say: "Not all black people are criminals, and not all criminals are black people."

# The Word Is Mightier Than the Stone

....................................................

*Leah Haider, age 18*

CRACK! THE SOUND OF BROKEN GLASS REVERBERATED THROUGH-out the quiet neighborhood. My heart sank somewhere between my knees and ankles. Then, out of the corner of my eye, I saw my friend start to ride away. I jumped on my bike as fast as I could and rock-eted off toward home. My heart was racing, and it felt like an eter-nity before I reached my house. I threw my bike down in the garage and slunk away to my room. For the rest of the afternoon I sat on my bed and cried. It felt like I had the weight of the world on my shoulders. This was my second day living in California; I wished I had never stepped off the plane.

I remember eating dinner that night as clear as a bell. Every time my mother would ask me a question, I felt like shouting out, "Yes, I broke the window!" However, I couldn't bring myself to say it, so I would just answer her question with a short yes or no. She knew that something was wrong, but she didn't say anything. I held in my secret as tight as I could, hoping it would somehow disappear.

I lasted about one more hour, and I couldn't take the guilt any-more. I went downstairs and bit the bullet. I told her about how I met Justin at the basketball court, and we decided to go biking. We had just turned the corner of Pizzoli Place when two kids started making fun of us. Then, one boy asked Justin why he was hanging out with a Chink. We stopped biking and just kind of stood there. The word stung my ears, and it felt like someone had stabbed me in the heart. I was infuriated, and I picked up a rock from the ground.

I was filled with an animal rage, and I launched the rock straight through the front window of the boys' house.

When I finished talking, I looked up at my mother like a dog that had been caught eating off the table. She wasn't mad. She understood that this was the first time anyone had ever made fun of me because of my race. She paid for the window, and we never talked about the incident again.

My family and I moved back to Minnesota when I was in junior high. The next time I heard a racial slur I was a freshman in high school. My friend started to date a boy who is Scandinavian, and she is Filipino. One day I heard him talking about those stinkin' gooks. I asked him if he knew that I was a gook. He said he knew that I was of Asian descent, but I wasn't a gook. I asked him why he didn't consider me a gook. His answer was simply, "Because you're Leah." I didn't know how to react to that, to be honest. I wanted to slap him, but he didn't insult me directly. He did insult my heritage, but I didn't know my heritage because I was adopted when I was six months old. I just tucked it away and never thought about it again.

Last summer, I started working at a local drugstore. It was my second day on the job when a man who was paying for his items asked, "Where are you from?" I answered that I was from Minnesota. He repeated, "No, where are you *from?*" I told him that I was originally from South Korea. That seemed to satisfy him, but it didn't satisfy me. I knew what he was really asking. He was asking, why aren't you white? Because if I were white, nobody would ask me where I was from. I get asked this question often, and it bothers me. I am a citizen of the United States of America, and I am no different from anybody else because I am Korean.

The next week I was watching television when I turned to a comedy show. Margaret Cho was on, and she was talking about how she reacted to a racial slur. A man called her a Chink, and this is how she responded: "Sir, I am not a Chink. I am a gook. If you're going to use a racial slur, make sure that you use the right one. You might offend somebody." All of a sudden, I flashed back to that day in California. I still remember the hurt feeling and how gorgeous it was outside. I could remember the smell of a barbecue in a neighbor's backyard. I couldn't help but laugh because that boy was Filipino, and he had called me a Chink. Now I realize that you can't change ignorant people, but you can change how you respond to them. I resolved that the next time somebody directs a racial slur toward me, I will fight them with words, not rocks.

# The Color on the Other Side of the Mirror

......................................................

*Lonnie Joseph, age 18*

I HAVE BEEN AFFECTED BY RACISM IN MANY DIFFERENT WAYS, sometimes verbally, sometimes by actions. Like they say, actions show louder than words.

When I was living in the U.S. Virgin Islands, people would talk about me and laugh. When I'd go walking, people would look at me and say, "She's so black, she looks like tar," or "Is Shaka Zulu your father?" Sometimes it hurt so bad that I would walk with my head to the floor. I knew my complexion was dark—I didn't need someone to tell me so. I could see myself in the mirror every day.

It wasn't just strangers who degraded me about my color. Even the people I called friends would joke. They'd say that if we were all in a dark room together, the only thing they would see was my teeth. They'd say that I'm so black that looking at me from afar, I look like darkness.

Boys don't like to be seen with me because they will be teased and called "tar baby." I've never had a male tell me I am beautiful or my color is perfect. Sometimes my self-esteem drops so low I don't care about anything.

Sometimes, people don't even want to sit next to me on the school bus, because they are afraid that some of my blackness will bounce off on them. I have never told anyone about this, but, one time, a girl told me that I didn't need a costume for Halloween because I was already dressed in black. I didn't let it bother me.

It's not only people my age. One day I was walking to the bus stop when I heard a lady say to her friend, "That girl is so black, I didn't see her just pass next to me." The thing that really hurt me was that the woman who said it was the same complexion as me, only a little lighter. I looked back at her and she said, "If you black, you just black." I asked her what color her skin was. She said, "I'm black, but you are the color itself." I just looked back at her and she laughed.

I tell myself that people see things and people say things; it's up to me to not let their words hurt me. But instead of building up my self-esteem, I find myself crying and wondering what's wrong with me.

The thing I have to remember is that racism isn't something we are born with. It's something we learn over time. I can't change the way the entire world feels, but each of us can change our own beliefs.

I see myself as a person of in-between beauty. I'm not saying that I am pretty or that I am ugly. I know that I am pretty in my own way, even though many people can't see this with their eyes. I may not look perfect, but I am perfectly fit. That's how I boost my self-esteem. It's what I tell myself at all times. I can't go to bed one color and get up to be another. I have to live and die with the darkness of my skin. It will never fade or rub off because of what people would like it to do.

I have learned that in order to love someone else's color, you have to see beyond black and white. Don't condemn people that are different from you. I know that I'm seen as a beast, but the real "beasts" are those people who act racist against you and me. The "beauties" are those who try their best to make us look past the word R-A-C-I-S-T. This is how I boost my self-esteem, so I am able to look forward to a new day.

# A Long Time Ago

...........................................................

*Harold T. Cribbs, Jr., age 17*

ONCE UPON A TIME I WAS YOUNG AND LIVING WITH MY PARENTS IN Maryland. I had a problem with all the kids in my neighborhood. All of them were white and older than I was. I didn't know why, but I didn't like them at all. I wouldn't go outside most of the time. Most of the time I didn't say anything to them, and they didn't say anything to me.

I was the kind who stayed in the house most of the time because I had no friends. Later that year I went to Florida for the summer and stayed with my aunt and uncle. I had a lot of fun, despite having to see all the white people. There were so many of them that I had no choice but to stay in the yard or in the house.

I knew that if I went outside, I would have to fight one or two of them just because of the way they looked at me. I was very mean then, but I guess I didn't like them because they were so different from me. Or was it because of the books I had read and the television I had watched where the black man was in chains and suffering?

I knew it was wrong to not like another person because of his or her color, but I didn't really care. I was just mad at the world, so I went on a long walk. I told my aunt and uncle I needed some time to myself. I left in anger. I was mad at a lot of things. I had to get a lot of stuff off my chest, so I started to walk. While walking, I found a clean lake. It was so hot outside that I just jumped in.

Time went by fast while I was chilling in the lake by myself, laid back, when a couple of kids came by and took my shirt. Then they started running and laughing. I said, "$#@! Come back here with my shirt." I got out of the water and ran after them. When I caught one of them, I almost killed him. He had to go to the hospital that same night.

I was at the police station. My uncle had to come get me out. He asked what happened and I told him the whole story, but he didn't care, and I wasn't sorry that I hurt that boy.

The next morning I was sent back home, and as soon as I got home I had to talk to my mother. She told me that all people are equal and no one is smarter or better. "God made everybody equal," she told me over and over again. I said, "Okay, Mother, we are equal, but it doesn't make us friends. I still don't like them." She said, "Boy, I didn't bring you up that way, to be hating other people because they look different than you. Boy, you better change and you better change fast." I said, "Okay, Mother." I decided I would change so conditions can change around the world. Maybe people would see me and follow my lead because things should change from the old days.

I thought about it a little more, and it made a lot of sense. I would change my ways so things could get better. That same day I went outside and made some friends with the white kids. They were not as bad as I thought they would be. One of the boys told me about slavery. He said that what they had done was wrong.

When I made my first white friend, I decided that they weren't all mean, just some of them were, but hopefully, they would change, too.

# Family Trouble

# Age Ten and Half-Empty, Age Seventeen and Half-Full

..............................................

*Anonymous, age 17*

GROWING UP IS DIFFICULT ENOUGH AS IT IS, BUT GROWING UP IN denial is even worse.

When my mom was pregnant with me, my father had an affair with another woman. This is what caused their divorce. My mom had to work five jobs, including a 3:00 to 11:00 shift at the hospital, just to make ends meet. I spent most of my childhood with my grandparents and my aunt. To this day, I remember how Mom would come to pick me up and buckle me in the backseat of her Cordoba. I was so tired, yet so anxious to see my mom. I saw how hard she worked to keep our house and to maintain a healthy environment for us.

When I was two, my mom met a man and fell in love. At first I called him Joe, then I called him Daddy Joe, and finally just Daddy. I was so young that I accepted him as my dad. My real father, Carl, had moved out West and remarried. He had two boys with his new wife, Natalie, so I had two new brothers. My stepmother convinced Carl to visit me on holidays.

On his visits, we would go to a truck lot and examine trucks and their parts. When you are young, you don't realize what you are doing; you just get excited about the people around you. I was so thrilled to see Daddy. Then, one day, the question came up: Why did I have two daddies?

As I grew older, I began to rebel against my mom and stepdad. I would overhear Mom saying that Carl hadn't paid his child support that week, or that he was $1,000 behind. I assumed that Mom and Joe were teaming up against Carl. I was confused; no one understood me or what I was feeling. But they never really said anything bad about Carl in front of me, and that was important.

When I was about ten years old, I realized that Carl wasn't always there for me when I needed him, and he didn't seem to care about what I was doing. When we talked on the phone, he would always ask, "How is science? How is music? Are you learning about geology yet?" I was ten years old—how did I even know what geology was? He didn't know me, never said that he was proud of me, and never said that he loved me. Joe, however, began to be the father I had always wanted. There was never a day that went by without him saying that he loved me.

I asked Carl one day why he didn't come see me very often and why he always asked me the same things when he saw me. He didn't have an answer. I was pained inside, because he couldn't be what I wanted him to be. I loved Joe, but deep down, I was confused. I wanted Carl to be where Joe was—in my home, married to my mom. I remember so many nights of tearing my room apart, throwing things, yelling at my mom and Joe, and crying hysterically. Then Carl would call and say something good to me and I would get sucked back in and love him again. I felt like a rag doll whose arms were constantly being tugged in different directions.

At age thirteen, when I began to mature, things started to change. I noticed that Carl was doing bad things. His parents were sick, and I thought that he should make a trip back home to help care for them. He never did. He would only visit when he was going to get something in exchange, like a gift for Christmas or his birthday. But no matter what Carl did, my grandparents couldn't see any fault in him. That killed me inside, because he was so wrong in so many ways. Nevertheless, I kept giving him another chance. I would say to myself,

"Oh, he just made a mistake, I love him, I want him to accept me, I know that he loves me."

Carl got another divorce and moved to the East Coast, where Natalie was already living. One summer, I went to visit Natalie and my brothers, and I planned to visit with Carl so we could discuss our relationship problems. We decided to go to the beach. The car was silent the whole way there, even though we hadn't seen each other in over a year. Finally, I broke the silence and asked, "Dad, why don't you ever show affection toward me?"

He hesitated and said, "Because when I see you, I see your mother, and I just can't show affection to that." Those were his exact words. I will never forget them; they have made a permanent scar on my heart. At that moment, I knew I hated this man. I hated him for having an affair with another woman and causing my mom so much pain, I hated him for never being there, and I hated him for being my father. I remained quiet; it seemed that my feelings couldn't come up—they were stuck deep down inside.

On the beach, Carl told me that he was dating a woman who had six children. He said that there was something else he needed to tell me. He then bluntly said, "Natalie is a lesbian. I caught her in bed one day with a woman when I came home unexpectedly. Also, your grandmother is an alcoholic." He told me these things as if I didn't care about these people, like he was trying to make them look bad. I began crying and yelled, "Stop Carl! Just stop! You have done enough damage, just stop!" Then I told him to take me home. When he dropped me off, I said I really didn't want to see or hear from him again, because I didn't want to be hurt anymore.

Two years went by, and I became so attached to Joe that he was "my dad." In 1995, Joe adopted me. Carl gave up his parental rights and handed them to Joe in exchange for owed and future child-support payments. That was the happiest day for my family and me. As far as a father-daughter relationship with Carl is concerned, there never was one and there never will be.

The support of my family helped me immensely. My mom let me visit Carl because she felt that I needed to make my own judgments about him. She stood back and allowed me to experience the realities of life, which proved to be both hurtful and beneficial. Once I realized the truth of my situation, I picked myself up by the bootstraps and told myself that only I could make a difference in my life.

Now, I feel that I can help my brothers by listening to them and talking with them about any paternal problems they may have. I coped with a difficult situation, and if my brothers ask me, I can try to help them cope, too. By listening, not judging, and keeping an open mind, I can help them through this difficult time in their lives.

In the past five years, I have learned that my grandmother was an alcoholic, my oldest brother has Tourette's syndrome and ADHD, and Natalie is a lesbian involved with an African-American woman named Andrea. I maintain an open relationship with Natalie, Andrea, and my brothers. Although it felt awkward at first, I knew that maintaining an open avenue of communication would be to my benefit. In fact, Natalie, Andrea, and the boys stayed at our house one weekend last year when they came up to go skiing. We ended up having a sing-along and telling family stories. I think my brothers understood that the most important thing in a family is love.

I feel content now with Natalie and Andrea. I know that they both really love the boys and me. I call them two or three times a month to update them on my latest adventures, and when I visit during the summer, we all enjoy each other's company. Through my visits and our monthly conversations, I am showing them—and myself—that I am satisfied with the situation.

# School of Hard Knocks

........................................

*MJBrooks, age 14*

I HAVE HAD MANY HARDSHIPS IN MY LIFE—NOT JUST SCHOOL AND my social life, but the loss of my father. Why did I lose him? He did not die; my parents got a divorce. According to an article in the October 3 issue of the *Denver Post,* statistics show that Colorado has the highest divorce rate in the country. Most of my friends' parents have either divorced and remarried or are single parents. So, why did this affect me so much? Perhaps because I never thought it would happen to me.

My parents seemed so happy together the first nine years of my life. I never heard them fight; and if they did, it was not made obvious to me. When I turned ten, we moved to Boulder so my father could finish his college degree. This is when the problems started, at least, that's what I believed. Most of the fighting and arguing occurred on the weekends, but as always, it was not obvious. When they went outside and came back indoors, they were always mad and never talked to each other. After that, I knew that my parents had a problem, but I didn't think this was the reason for their conflicts. When I asked what was wrong, I was silenced. I felt aloof, and I tried to avoid the signs of my father's alcoholism, even at the early age of eleven.

At age twelve, I attended my dad's family reunion. I remember how much fun it was sitting and talking to my aunts, uncles, and cousins. I also remember my father always hanging around the beer cooler, pulling out a beer every time I sat on his lap. I remember the gossip, the smells of the hamburgers and hot dogs on the grill, and the alcohol on his breath as we walked to the car.

Eventually, after a bunch of crazy little stories my dad told, we left the gathering. Again, my father continued to share his lousy stories as we hit the highway and my mom drove us back home. I recall my dad asking my mom to pull over, but she was not fast enough, and he began throwing up like a mad man. Was this because he was sick, maybe with a bad case of the flu? Or was he experiencing this nausea from intoxication? As usual, I was in denial and did not think of it as a problem.

Later that year, I thought things were settling down. The spring of his college graduation was wonderful. He finally received his college degree, and my mother seemed content to not have to deal with his alcoholic behavior anymore. My dad and I shared some precious moments together. We often went to the mall and talked about what was going on with me and about life in general. We ate lots of ice cream at Ben and Jerry's and Häagen-Dazs. But we were in for a drastic change.

In March, my parents decided that their marriage was over, not only because of the drinking, but also because of a brief affair that ended their relationship. They were officially divorced in December. I was so hurt that, at age thirteen, I decided to take action. I started smoking, not knowing that this would never bring back my father or get his attention. I gave my mother so much stress that she made me move in with my grandparents. I had no idea why I was smoking until my mother made me realize what I was doing. When she told my dad what was going on, his response was, "Deal with her! She's your daughter. I don't have time for her on top of my schedule!" My dad called back the next day to apologize to my mom, but I didn't care anymore. I had so much anger inside of me that I started to punish myself. I became obsessed with piercing my body, fighting with my mother, and thinking about suicide.

Now that I'm fourteen, I feel that all those things that went through my head were stupid. I regret going through those changes because of my dad. My father still hasn't changed; unfortunately, he still drinks. This summer I went to the zoo with my dad for a family picnic. I remember him talking to the animals and cussing them out. At the time I thought it was hilarious, because I've never seen him act quite like that. Although my dad was highly intoxicated, we talked and I realized it was easier to talk to him when he was drunk. When he is sober, it's harder to talk to him without him becoming easily stressed out and impatient. Oddly enough, I like him better drunk at times.

I think my father made some poor decisions that could have been fixed, but he decided to take matters into his own hands because of what he did in his past. However, we cannot change the past, or even his past. Therefore, I have to live life to the fullest. Even though it hurts.

> *We may not like people*
> *because of their flaws or*
> *immaturities, but the further*
> *we ourselves grow, the more*
> *we become able to accept-to*
> *love-them,*
> *flaws and all.*
>
> —Daily Reflections

# Everyone Has Their Own Story

........................................

*Claudia K., age 17*


EVERYBODY HAS THINGS TO COMPLAIN ABOUT FROM THEIR CHILD-hood. Everyone has at least one bad memory. Everyone wants to be felt sorry for at times. But if we accept our problems as just a part of life, we won't feel ashamed, and we won't influence our own children to stuff their feelings inside. If you talk about things and offer advice and want to change patterns, you will look back on your life and see that it wasn't as bad as it seemed—and you'll know that there is *always* room for change.

My story, I hope, will give someone something to learn from or help them know they're not alone. I guess I could begin by saying that the circumstances of my childhood made it terrible. We were poor, I was molested at the age of five, and my dad is an alcoholic. I was not "popular" in school because of my height and my glasses, and because when I breathe I wheeze heavily from huge tonsils and adenoids. I'm not going to start that way though. It wasn't as bad as it could have been. Things could have been much worse, but, at the time, it sure didn't feel like it. My brother and my dad started to fight really bad when I was about nine. They would get into huge arguments right in front of my face and it would end up with them fistfighting and my mom refereeing out in the front yard. It would end with my brother screaming obscenities to my mom and dad and then running away for a few days. I didn't understand why they fought so much. I always knew that my brother wasn't my dad's biological son, but was that the reason? All that resentment. I still don't know to this day.

My dad—he's a great guy. He's funny and nice and he acts like a teenager. But there are reasons for that. He is immature. He married my mom, who was a single mother with my brother, and a year later they had me. He always drank. He is yet another victim of the disease of alcoholism. He also has a drug problem. I have known about all of this since I was a little girl. Dealing with an alcoholic has been hell. It ruins lives and families and dreams, and, after a few times of rehab not working, you slowly begin to lose your respect for and hope in that person. But my dad has so many issues he hasn't dealt with that he doesn't realize what he's really like. He has these massive mood swings from strict, selfish, and screaming, to nice, funny, and caring. I think he's a manic depressive. I know schizophrenia runs in my family. My dad uses chemicals to run away from his problems, just like so many other people these days.

So my life surrounding "men" hasn't been all that great. Ever since I was abused I have never been the same. The word "man" terrified me for years. I am just now starting to get more comfortable around guys, even my dad. Therapy has helped a little, but I never really cared for counselors. I know that what happened has made me more independent, and I trust myself more now than ever. I won't let any man take control or overpower me. Unfortunately, this has pushed many guyfriends away. That is probably one of the main reasons I have stayed a virgin, but that's also a moral issue for me. I can't help the way I feel, but I still have to learn that falling in love won't make me weak, only stronger.

My mama—she is a great lady. She was depressed for a while, but then she got the help she needed and finally became strong enough to take her life into her own hands. I think I have learned my feminist independence from her. She has always supported me in everything, and even when she didn't, she trusted me enough to know that I knew how to make my own decisions and that I could take care of myself. She let me grow up fast. I will always love her for that. My dad and brother, on the other hand, still think of me as the little girl I used to be. I always tell my mom how much I hate it.

It's as if I am not respected for my own ideas and no one listens to what I have to say.

My mom made a huge decision the fall of my senior year. She decided to get a divorce from my dad. I had no idea what was happening. I couldn't believe it. I wanted them to separate because all they did was fight, and all dad and I could do was argue. I got real sick of it, fast.

My mom saw that I was starting to have serious anxiety attacks and she got me into therapy again. I started taking antidepressants and slowly began to feel better. I was crushed seeing my dad move out. I loved him, but I just couldn't live with him anymore. While all this was going on, I had been busy with school. I was in numerous plays and other extracurricular activities. My grades slipped again, but I think college will be good for me. I will be able to get away and start over. At least there is one goofy thing that has come from this whole situation—my mom and I have grown stronger together. We need each other, and we are always there for each other. My brother and I still need some work on our relationship, but with time, we will become close friends, I'm sure.

Still, with everything that has gone on, I know that I am a strong person. All the terrible things that have happened to me have taught me how true this saying is: "That which does not kill us, makes us stronger." I live by that motto. I have made bad choices and suffered greatly for it, but it's not my parents' fault. I choose my own behavior in the long run. I'm determined to be the first kid in my family to go to college. I have stayed responsible in all the activities I am in, such as a peer mediation group, which helps kids deal with their problems. I am also in two singing groups and I take voice lessons. I am active in the theater program at our school, I write poetry, and I am a member of a chemical-free group. I hope someday that my decisions and actions will make me a good role model for someone. Well, everyone has their own story. I have mine; you have yours. Our lives are all different, and we all have the right and chance to succeed.

# BODY IMAGE

# Challenging Anorexia

.........................................................

*Gianna Cardinale, age 14*

I'VE FACED MANY CHALLENGES IN THE PAST, BUT DURING MY eighth-grade year, as I blew on my candle of life, I was never prepared to face the challenge of saving my own life.

It started as a simple diet. The perfectionist in me wanted my hips to melt away and my "rosebud" breasts to vanish, so I'd have a model's "perfect" body. It was September when my best friend told me, "Just promise me you won't become anorexic." I blew her off, telling her that I had enough control to stop as soon as I was thin enough, but I was wrong. By then, there were two voices in my brain, the anorexic and the old me. Unfortunately, the old me was a mere raisin compared to the anorexic that was now in control.

On a typical day, I would eat half a banana, half a cup of yogurt, and half a veggie dog—200 calories, compared to the 2000-plus calories that my growing body needed. I was taken to doctors, psychologists, and dietitians, all of whom helped for a few days, at least. But I would always end up cheating the meal plans and slacking off on the quantities. Not because I wanted to, but because the anorexia kept tugging me down a long tunnel where I had no sense of reason. I constantly thought I was overweight. It seemed that if I could eat less than what the meal plan required, then I wouldn't have to feel guilty about eating too much. I would turn a half cup of cottage cheese into a quarter cup, then an eighth of a cup, then two tablespoons. I thought I was proud of that, but it was really the anorexic that was proud, because it was winning control of my mind.

My weight kept dropping until, at sixty pounds, I could hardly conceive of what a normal life was like anymore. I backed away from people, I stopped giving and receiving love. I vaguely remember coming home each day, sitting in front of the fire, scorching my paper-thin skin and scalding my untasting mouth with boiled tea in an attempt to keep warm. My nails grew thin and brittle, my hair thinned and receded, and a disgusting fuzz grew all over my bony body (a natural reaction by the body in an effort to keep warm). One night, I woke up with my mom huddled around me. She was afraid that my heart would stop in my sleep.

Despite all of this, I was such a zombie that I didn't realize how much I was hurting not only myself, but the people around me. My sister grew scared when I tried to exercise, my dad cried when he saw me, and my friends had to see the school counselor. People called to ask my mom what was wrong with me, but I could never understand why. Each time I found out that I'd lost more weight, I would feel so sad that I'd promise to gain it back soon, but because of my lack of nutrition, a third of my brain was not available for reasoning. The anorexia was too strong for my weak soul, making me lie and hurt myself.

Each day I thought, "If I starve today, then I'll be extra thin and ready to eat tomorrow." The next day, I'd be back on the treadmill of starvation, cutting back even more, challenging myself to see how pathetically thin I could become. And yet, I cherished every minute I spent eating. I tried to get other people to eat all the foods that I wouldn't, so I could have the satisfaction of watching them eat.

Christmas came and went, and my face was so thin that it looked like my eyes had been punched in and bruised. My hip bones popped out, my ribs could be counted. I got a big scab where my tailbone had rubbed against the chair. I'd wake up in the morning with bruises from my bones rubbing against my skin. My breath was stale; it reeked of rotting stomach acid. This wasn't the glamorous, thin life I had expected to enjoy. Nevertheless, I thought I looked just fine. I wondered how so many kids at school knew that I had an eating disorder. Some of the ruder boys would scream at me, "Why don't you just eat a cow?" but I didn't get it. Why were people so mean?

Finally, in January, my new psychiatrist, a highly-acclaimed specialist on eating disorders, informed me that I weighed sixty pounds and had a temperature of 92°F (hypothermia level). My body was so hungry that it was eating away at my kidneys, brain, and heart. He needed to admit me to a hospital before fatal damage was done. I was scared, but not enough to give in. Student council elections were coming up that next week, and I was running for Vice President. He finally agreed to let me remain at home—on the condition that I ate everything my parents fed me. On Monday, he'd decide whether or not I still needed hospitalization.

That first weekend was one of the worst weekends of my life. I was forced to eat the foods that I'd feared for so long: beef chili, grilled cheese sandwiches, peanut butter, one-percent milk, eggs, toast with butter, pork, beef stew, mayonnaise, and pancakes. I hated my parents for torturing me. How could they do this to me? They knew how much I hated red meat and fat, but they wouldn't give in.

At each meal, I screamed and cried. My sister would leave the room, but my loving parents stuck with their job. They kept me out of the hospital, which I can now greatly appreciate.

My doctor said that I could stay at home, but I had to remain supervised at all times. At school, my parents fed me lunch and the nurses monitored my snacks at locker break. I wasn't allowed to exercise at first, but I snuck into the bathroom to do jumping jacks, until I was caught. Somehow, though, I managed to pull myself together for elections—and win!

Weeks went by and my parents still monitored all my meals. It felt odd not being able to feed myself. Even if I wanted something extra to eat, I wouldn't let myself, fearing the next dreadful meal ahead. Each week at group therapy, I complained about how much I had to eat until, finally, a recovered patient asked me, "Do you want to get better, or be anorexic for years?" That's when I realized that instead of letting anorexia win, I could actually try to enjoy eating and getting well.

The change in my thinking was amazing, and I still attribute it to the fact that I was becoming renourished. I stopped hiding pieces of snacks in my pocket when the nurses weren't looking. I didn't exercise every spare minute, and I stopped arguing at meal times. I began to think positively instead of negatively. I was going to gain back my weight anyway, so why prolong it?

I kept myself going by setting goals that, because of my perfectionist personality, I knew I'd reach. My parents promised to buy me many new clothes as soon as I'd outgrown my size-ten children's clothes, which I had worn back in the fourth grade. There were also the rewards of serving myself, eating out with my friends, eating what I chose, and looking my age—healthy, not scrawny. Nevertheless, each day was a struggle to run that extra mile, eat that extra piece of cheese. I wanted to get better, but the illness kept tugging me back.

After I had taken that first step, I began to laugh about how much olive oil my dad put in our food. I thanked my parents for their delicious cooking. I told other members in the group how red meat had really helped my recovery. Soon, positive behavior began to pay off. Our family was happier. I became the recovery miracle in group therapy. I was granted the privilege of eating lunch at school twice a week—unsupervised—with my friends. Eating became enjoyable! I even began to get hungry for my morning, afternoon, and evening snacks, though I never would have admitted it.

I was overjoyed the day my parents finally agreed to let me spend the night at a friend's house. My friend and I went out to breakfast the next morning. I looked at the menu and ordered the right things: eggs, toast, a bowl of fruit, and milk. After we paid the bill, my friend looked at my plate. Seeing my milk unfinished and two strawberry slices leftover, she said maturely, "Gianna, we're not leaving until you've finished everything." Thankful for friends who cared so much about me, I complied with her request. Later, I had the experience of losing my best friend. Maybe she was sick of the illness. I sure was.

April was rolling around, and I faced the problem of the Washington, D.C., trip that I had signed up for in the fall. Fortunately, my psychiatrist convinced my parents that I was well enough to go.

The trip turned out to be fun, and though I didn't gain any weight, I didn't lose any, either. Instead of avoiding food, I was actually eating much bigger meals than the other kids. I'd pack snacks for the bus, and I'd make sure to get a turkey sandwich and milk or a bag of trail mix before bedtime. This must have shown my parents that I was healing. Soon I was allowed to feed myself almost all of my snacks and meals, though they still checked on me to make sure that I was doing a good job, which I was. I'd get up at the crack of dawn to cook myself an omelet, hash browns, and oatmeal. Instead of exercising furiously, I'd walk the dogs or play tennis.

Though I was eating about 2500 calories, my metabolism had become so high that my weight wouldn't budge from eighty-five pounds. I was solid muscle. Many people asked if I was a gymnast or a runner. Though I was still very thin, I thought that I looked normal, and I didn't want to increase my food intake.

Several weeks before graduation, Mom gave me a new challenge: If I gained back all my weight, we'd buy new dresses for graduation and the dance. Being in love with clothes, I decided that I could gain the weight back.

It was hard to increase my food intake. I started by adding a piece of toast to a snack of fruit and yogurt, or beans and Canadian bacon to my already large breakfast. And I still didn't gain weight! I grew so frustrated that I decided to eat until I was completely full. The amount of food it took to fill me up was incredible. After school, I'd eat a huge snack, followed by a huge dinner. Before I went to bed, I'd be hungry again, so I'd eat a BIG snack before bed. I thought I would gain ten pounds in a week, but I didn't gain anything. Still, my mom bought me the dresses for my effort.

Throughout the summer I began to lose my fear of food completely. I reached over 4000 calories a day. The best part was that it was my decision to gain the weight—I was the one who chose to eat that much. I was amazed at how hard it was to gain weight, but it slowly came back as solid muscle. About mid-summer, I looked like my old self. I felt great, and since I have a summer birthday, I was delighted that I could eat pizza and ice-cream cake on my birthday, without freaking out.

This year has been fabulous so far; I have wonderful friends and a great social life, as well as challenging honors classes. I made varsity tennis, ran in a 12K race, and learned some challenging piano pieces. My appetite is hearty—I eat large quantities of food, and I'm not afraid of getting fat anymore.

Since I have overcome the challenge of anorexia, I feel I can do anything. I am a happier, more confident person now. I'd much rather have my healthy, muscular body than a thin, ineffective body, which goes to show that sometimes you don't know how great something is until you've lost it. I don't stress out very often anymore. I know that I'm capable of achieving anything I set out to do. I don't have to prove to the world that I'm perfect. The most important thing that I've learned from a year of anorexia is that it doesn't matter what a person looks like on the outside, as long as they're secure and confident with their inner self. I love life, no matter what hurdles lie ahead.

# Shrimp

*B.J., age 13*

A SHRIMP. THAT'S WHAT I AM. THINK ABOUT IT. AN ITSY-BITSY teeny-weenie crustacean that you can buy by the pound and cook thirty different ways. Not the most worshiped creature in the animal kingdom. Yet it is an amazingly appropriate name for a person who, because of size, is almost rock bottom on the human "food chain." Shrimps are the providers for other people's needs. We live in a society that thinks the bigger and stronger you are, the higher in our culture you should be. I personally don't think the modern community should act like a pride of lions when deciding who should have the most power. (Living in an eighth-grade commonwealth, I have learned that because of this attitude, respect comes at a greater cost. Therefore, it is more cherished once attained.)

Living at the expense of others' crude and often pointless "humor" can both strengthen and weaken a person's emotional state. One of the worst parts about the consistent bombardment of taunts and jokes is that most of the people who poke fun (except the truly mean at heart) would never think of doing anything like that to one of their buddies.

It's not always just what people say, but sometimes what they do. Being a pygmy, I am considered vulnerable, which makes me an easy target for anybody who wants to dump their sorrow or depression on someone else. I'm more prone to physical threats and the always-present "I'm better than you" attitude. Hardly a week goes by that I'm not verbally belittled by some adult who thinks I'm a fourth or fifth grader. That is one reason why restaurants are so unappealing to me. No matter where I go, I always get handed the kiddy menu and crayons. Sure, an eighth grader would say, "Um, I think I would wike da beenie-weenies and a smaw gwass of miwk." Come on, I don't even like beenie-weenies! There have been a few remarks that have truly hurt my feelings, but usually I can just make a joke so people are laughing with me and not at me.

The first time I really noticed I was short was picture day in kindergarten. The day before, we had to practice lining up to make class pictures easier the next day. I was second to last. I was taller than a girl, just barely, who I remember was kind of cute. She and I shared the same birthday. (How I remember this, I will never know.) Anyway, when picture day came, she fixed her hair into a miniature beehive, making her two or three inches taller than me. I remember wishing I could do that with my hair. The same thing happened every year (not the part about the hair). I was the smallest in the class until, I think, the third grade. How's that for stimulating a child's psychological growth? Yet, even after three or four years of being the shortest in the class, I didn't think I would always be undersized. It just didn't click. After second grade, just before we moved, I thought I was normal size and everyone in the school was tall. It wasn't really put into perspective until picture day (again). Yes, I was still diminutive.

Now that I am in middle school, there are no class pictures. For once, picture day isn't so demeaning or traumatic. Don't get me wrong; the process is logical, it's just not very appealing to an eighth grader who is almost fourteen and isn't even five feet tall.

I end up forgetting instances like these in a matter of hours, so I can just get along with my day. Other accounts, like the next one, really hurt my feelings, and I can't overlook them that easily.

When I was nine, I took part in a Tae Kwon Do tournament. It was the sparring portion of the competition. I never was that good at sparring, but for some reason I was really doing well that day. I had won my previous matches and was about to spar for first place with a kid I had fought (and lost to) earlier in practice.

He always thought that since he was larger, by at least five or six inches, he would beat me every time, which he did. Anyway, after the match, the judges declared me the winner. I was so happy, because I had never won first place in sparring. Then I heard my opponent tell his father that he had let me win, because I was "too small" for him to fight. It was just like monsoon season, right in the middle of my parade.

Even though being vertically challenged is a burden, without it, I may never have reached the intellectual status in which I currently reside. When I was a toddler, people thought I was brilliant when they saw my accomplishments. I was just slightly advanced, but my size magnified their perceptions of my abilities. I think because I constantly heard something to the effect of, "Look at that little guy go, he is really smart," I gained a high level of confidence in my academic abilities.

Even though I would like to be more elevated (my New Year's resolution always consists of growing several inches), I have learned to accept my size, along with everything else I know I can't change. Everything that I can control, however, I try to improve on.

So no matter who you are, your strengths outnumber your weaknesses. Every challenge you have faced has probably helped you in some grand way. You really don't have to be tall to aim high and reach your goals. I know that being small is a minute problem in the big scope of the world (what with nuclear weapons and hostile extraterrestrials who are ready to take over the earth). I also know that I should be thankful that I don't have a deceased parent or a prosthetic limb. But this is my problem, and I am overcoming it.

# The Lying Mirror

*A.C.B., age 15*

I STILL DON'T KNOW EXACTLY WHAT DROVE ME TO THE CONCLU-
sion, but at 5 feet 5 inches tall and 112 pounds, I decided I was fat.
I was a bright, vibrant, cute, popular, and very happy thirteen-year-
old girl with no real problems. My parents were happily married, I
got along well with my younger sister, and we had a secure, stable
family life. Looking back now, I believe that the pressures from the
media, peers, and the "perfectionist, first-born" in me worked
together to drive me to anorexia.

What started out as "only a few pounds" grew into a weight-loss
hell. My diet started in March 1995, and by the end of June of that
year, I had dropped from 112 pounds to 87. In the beginning, my
friends complimented me on how good I looked, and that only
fueled my weight loss campaign. It was after a week spent at summer camp in June, where I had lost ten pounds by eating very little
while burning lots of calories walking up and down hills all week,
that my mom began to take notice of the significant difference in
my appearance.

I now realize I had a disease, because the more I lost, the more
unhappy I became and the more I "had" to lose more weight. I
became gaunt, cranky, moody, and tired. In fact, for about six
months, it was almost like I was in a coma. A close relative died in
the summer of 1995, and I truly don't remember anything about it.
My mom told me I didn't show any emotion at the funeral, and others noticed it. All I could think about was food. It was an all-con-
suming nightmare. My weight dropped even further, and I became a
walking skeleton. The friends who had previously complimented me

on my weight loss were now telling me I was too skinny. My size-3 jeans hung loosely from my now frail frame. I was no longer happy or vibrant, and I rarely smiled anymore. My stomach ached twenty-four hours a day with gnawing hunger pains. While I forced myself to exercise several hours a day, I was growing weaker physically, mentally, and emotionally. Whenever I looked in the mirror, I still saw a "fat" person, no matter how skinny I got. As I reflect back on this time, I now realize that as an anorexic, you have no life, just a living hell.

My road to recovery was slow and difficult. At first I refused to admit I was an anorexic. I resisted anyone helping me and hated people who made me eat. I made excuses so I wouldn't have to go to parties and dinners. I hated eating in public. My mirror kept lying to me, telling me I was fat, while my scale registered a skeletal eighty-three pounds. I kept my gaunt weight of eighty-three pounds for about a year.

Slowly, with the help of my parents and literature on anorexia, I got it through my head that I should gain some weight. As I mentioned earlier, during the lowest depths of my illness, it was like I was in a coma. I remember very little of the beginning of my road to recovery. My mom remembers my journey more clearly as we first came to grips with the true nature of my illness. She sent for literature, read articles in magazines and books, and confronted me with the reality of it all, naming it for what it was—anorexia. This was a difficult but crucial point for us all. She recalls that at first I would not even discuss it, but she left earmarked information for me to read on my own. I began to read about my disease and the damage it was doing to me. My mother said that some part of my numb brain realized that if I kept up the way I was going, I could actually die. I spent hours with my parents discussing the nature of my illness, how I acquired it, and a plan for recovery. I, personally, recall very little of this process or these discussions.

With a growing fear of the future I faced, along with the literature I read and the discussions I had with my parents, it got through to me that I should gain some weight. I didn't want to, but I gradually began to eat more. I didn't gain much weight for a few months. Then, all of a sudden, I shot up to ninety-six pounds! I got scared that I was going to get even "fatter." I went back to my diet to lose the weight, but it just made me gain more. I became a basket case. My fight with food and my weight grew even worse when I got back up to 112 pounds. I hated myself—I thought I was huge! I now had to wear size-5 jeans (which still were loose) and my mirror revealed a grossly gigantic person. My friends told me how good I looked now and I acted like everything was okay, even though I was still at constant war with myself. I was unhappy and angry with myself for "losing control" of my body. Whenever I saw myself in mirrors I had the haunting, constant thought, "I'm *so* fat!"

Now, almost three years later, I'm still at war with myself. Although I've reached a healthy weight and follow a balanced diet and exercise program, I still think I'm fat. I see anorexia as similar to alcoholism and drug addiction, where one is never really "cured," but only at various stages of the recovery process. I have come to accept this. I still suffer from the effects and mind-set of anorexia and probably always will.

Some positive habits have resulted from my struggles. I eat a balanced, healthy diet and don't fall into the junk food traps many of my peers do. I realize the importance of physical fitness and exercise and incorporate a healthy routine into my lifestyle. I have become a very good cook and do most of the cooking, baking, and grocery shopping for our family. I wish I could say that I have a magic formula for recovery from anorexia. I wish I could say I have met the challenge and conquered it. In truth, it continues to be a daily struggle.

My advice? For all teens, preteens, and their moms: Stop the obsession with weight. I am constantly aware of how many conversations center on weight and the presumed need for weight loss. "How much does so-and-so weigh?" "Oh! I'm *so fat!*"—this spoken mostly by underweight girls and women.

My advice for the anorexic: Accept yourself the way you are. Understand that, during the teen years, your body is changing a lot. A few years of being skinny in junior and senior high isn't worth the hell of the often devastating long-term effects you'll have to live with the rest of your life as a result of succumbing to this disease. I am constantly reminded by my parents that I am a unique, talented, beautiful girl, created in the image of God, with a purpose in life just as I am.

# Loving Myself

........................

*CJJ, age 18*

I'M NOT SURE EXACTLY WHEN I FIRST BEGAN STUDYING MYSELF IN that dreadful mirror and telling myself that I was ugly. I know that it didn't just suddenly happen one day. It was many small things, building up over many years. Everyone telling my sister how pretty she was, while neglecting to tell me anything. Guys going for the "pretty," "popular" girls at school and ignoring me. All those beautiful models and actresses that looked back at me every time I turned the channel or walked down a magazine aisle.

I hated every part of my body. Especially my face. Oh, all those hours I spent in front of the mirror, behind that closed bathroom door, picking out exactly what made me ugly. My nose was too big, one eye slants to the side. I have to wear glasses, my top teeth are crooked, and so on. Sometimes, when I was alone in the house, I would scream out "You're ugly! I hate you!" and then I would cry.

I spent many nights, alone in my room, crying, telling myself how ugly I was. I felt worthless. I would listen to love songs and tell myself that no guy would love someone as ugly as me. No guy would ever love me, period. I wasn't worth being loved.

I was spiraling downward. I was headed toward rock bottom, and quickly. I felt alone, isolated. I thought that no one would understand how I felt, what I was going through on the inside. So I hid it behind an empty smile and jokes. No one knew how I felt about myself, especially not my parents. They were the last ones I would expect to understand. I knew that they would tell me that I was being ridiculous and that I was beautiful. And when they did tell me that I was beautiful, I blew it off, knowing that's what all parents tell their daughters. That's what parents are supposed to tell you. I didn't even believe my friends, reasoning that they were only saying it because they were my friends. So I blew off what they told me and went home and told myself how ugly I was.

One night, as I lay alone in my room, I thought of how I could end it all. I planned it all out in my head. The next time I was alone, I would take a bath. Then I would slit my wrists, both of them, with a razor, and die. Suicide. I would end it all. All the pain. All the suffering that I felt inside. I scared myself so hard that I cried for hours.

After that I knew things had gone too far. I had to help myself, and fast. So I began to talk to a girl in school, a new friend of mine, who had gone through, was going through, what I was. I confessed it all to her. We supported each other whenever the other needed it. We shared stories and did things together that made us feel beautiful. We gave ourselves makeovers, bonded over "chick flicks," and argued over who was the cutest guy we knew. She helped me to see how pretty I was and how to love myself. And she introduced me to my first boyfriend. When I was with him I felt so beautiful. His words of "you're pretty" and "I love you" helped me to better love myself, inside and out. He was wonderful and helped me through some tough times.

The battle that I fight will never truly end. I know that. Some days I feel as if I'm on top of the world. I look in the mirror and see a beautiful girl staring back at me. I see me, and I feel good about myself. Then there are days when I crash down, cry, and look in the mirror and say that I'm ugly. But now, with the help of my friends, I can get back up again. I can go on. I can survive.

I have a self-confidence now that I never had before. I wear clothes that show off my body. I flirt with guys; I've even asked a few out. I notice now that guys look at me because I have confidence, I have higher self-esteem. And you know what? That's the best feeling in the world when a guy checks you out. I've even had guys lose their balance and run into the side of a bridge while watching me. That's just another self-confidence boost. If I was so ugly, then they would never look at me that way. Never. But they do look at me. So I must be attractive. I must be pretty. No, I must be beautiful. Yes, I am beautiful. I always was.

So, no, the battle never ends, but, yes, it gets easier with each passing day. It really does. All you have to do is look into that mirror (no, not that dreadful mirror, that wonderful mirror) and tell yourself that you are pretty, inside and out. I'm pretty for being who I am. I know that you've heard it before and that you don't believe it, but true beauty does come from within.

Whatever you do, just don't keep it all bottled up inside. Tell someone, anyone, how you feel. Tell a friend, a counselor, a parent, or anyone you can trust who can help you. Tell them everything, and let them help you. When they tell you how beautiful and pretty you are, listen to them. They're right. You are pretty and beautiful. You really are.

The battle is never over, but you can win it. I know that I'm winning and I know that you will win too. Just believe in yourself.

# IMMIGRANT EXPERIENCE

# Escape

*Patty Vodenka, age 18*

MY NAME IS PATTY AND I LIVE IN MINNESOTA. I JUST REALIZED that some people don't understand. They think that immigrants are bad for our country. Some are, but there are others who come to make life better for their families.

Like my father, who came to America with two suitcases, one sleeping bag, a wife, and two kids. My father hated it in Czechoslovakia (now known as the Czech Republic). He didn't like the Communists telling people what to think and what to do. He didn't want his children growing up in such an overpowering world, such a horrible life. So he told my mom, even before they were married, that one day he would go to America and be free. It was a dream a lot of people shared, but not too many accomplished.

On June 17, 1983, my family accomplished this dream. We went to visit our cabin on the Vitava River. We often went to our cabin, so my grandparents, aunts, and uncles thought it was nothing more than an average trip. We couldn't tell anybody that we were planning to escape, because someone might try to stop us. If the government found out, they might have put us in jail. Then we never would have been free.

Fog flowed over the river. There was a quiet swish of the water as it lightly waved against the rocks of the cliffs. The moonlight flowed over the trees and into the window of our small, one-room cabin. Dad was out putting the bags in our little blue European car. He packed everything we could take with us. It was quiet in the forest. As I slept, I dreamt that my brother, Peter, and I were swimming in the river. I inhaled the sweet smell of the forest, when a whisper called to me. I slowly left the river and returned to the small room. I hesitantly opened my eyes. My mom leaned over me, whispering "It's time to go, Patty. Get up." I sat up. Next to me, my brother woke up whining. I looked around the small, cozy room. A few oil lamps were lit, hanging from the wall. As my eyes adjusted to the light, I looked around and saw all the drawings and carvings my grandfather had done. I did not know that this would be the last time I would see these wonderful creations.

I looked out the window. It was still dark. I was confused; it was too early to go anywhere. My mom handed us some buttered bread and a glass of water. After we ate, she helped us get dressed. Dad came in. "Hurry," he whispered, then he left again.

We finished our bread, blew out the candles, and rushed to the car. My dad turned around and looked one last time at the dark river and the shadowy cliffs. The run-down old cabin stood lifeless. I didn't think about it then, but now I understand. My father grew up in that cabin. It was the most beautiful place in the world.

Once in the car, Peter and I fell asleep. We slept most of the way. A few hours later, my mom woke us. It was raining. She frantically got us into our raincoats, but since she couldn't reach us from the front seat, she had to come around and open the door. My mom wouldn't let me take my umbrella, or even my doll. I complained, of course, because my umbrella was pretty and it was raining. The trunk closed and my dad ran up behind my mom. "Quick," he said in a panicked voice, "They know we are here and they are coming." My mom pulled my brother out of the car and gave him to my dad. She dragged me out next and didn't bother to close the door. I stopped and waited for my mom to get a bag out of the car. My dad and brother started running.

I saw the doors swing open on an old, gray, run-down cement building. Dogs were barking, men were yelling. My mom grabbed my hand, and we took off after my dad and brother. They were already a good distance in front of us. In the dark, we couldn't see which way they went. My dad called to us to follow the sound of his voice.

We were running for our lives, not knowing what was going to happen. Not even knowing if we were running in the right direction. My heart was pounding, my little chubby legs running as fast as a four-year-old's could. I was slipping on the mud, splashing in the puddles. We were running into a black hole. Flashlights from behind us and gunfire in front of us lighted our way. I could hear feet splashing through the puddles. The dogs barked.

Then there was a scream somewhere up ahead. We kept running, not knowing if my dad and brother were hurt or even dead. We kept running into the darkness, not knowing how far we had gone, how far we had to go. Not knowing if they were going to catch or shoot us, like so many they had caught and killed before us.

Something appeared on the ground in front of us. It looked like a body. My dad? Oh, god, no—a bag. My mom was freaked. I guess she wanted to pick it up but didn't have time. Then the ground disappeared and we stumbled down a hill. I heard the water before I saw the creek. My mom picked me up by one arm and made her way slowly, dragging me across the water without being able to see just where she was stepping.

Once we got to the other side, we started up another hill. Flashlights shone down on us. Slipping, my mom pulled me up the muddy hill. As I turned my head, I saw beams of light and the shadows of men. The dogs still barked.

My mom ran faster because she knew they had a clear shot at us. We got to the top, then dashed into the dark woods before us. Black shadows reached for us, trying to hold us back. My mom was tangled in branches that held her like barbed wire. I looked back again; the flashlights shone through the trees. "Mom, they are coming," I whispered. I pulled on her, but instead of pulling her out, I ended up getting pulled in. I thought my eyes were closed, it was so dark. Finally, struggling blindly, we got out and started forward again, hoping we were going the right way. We moved quickly, but not too quickly. Then it was dark.

We looked around. What had happened? The flashlights. The flashlights had disappeared. Were the men going to sneak up on us? We had to be careful, moving quickly but quietly, so they wouldn't find us. Was it a trick? Were we supposed to think that they were gone, that we could slow down or stop, and then they would catch us? We hurried to get away. My dad's voice called out to us in the forest. We followed it.

After walking for some time, we made it to the edge of the forest, where we found my dad and brother. We were in some kind of field. My mom laid down the sleeping bag for Peter and me. We stood, frozen, wet, and very tired, waiting for my mom to get the sleeping bag ready. It turned out that the yelling was my dad falling down into the creek. "I think the creek was the border," he said. My brother and I got out of our wet clothes and climbed into the sleeping bag. As I drifted off to sleep, I thought about what we had just been through, and I knew that I would never forget it.

Later that morning, my parents woke us. We walked over to some nearby houses. We were now in Austria. My brother and I were still wet. We had no dry clothing because my dad had dropped the bag. My dad ended up going back over the border to get the bag with the clothes. This was dangerous, because it was light now and he could have easily been caught.

We waited for my dad's friends, who had escaped before us, to come pick us up and take us away from the border of the world we had left behind. Sitting in the morning sun, we heard a noise that we had never heard before. It was a moose. The moose was looking out from the forest, screaming, as if it were telling us we were free. I remember this well—it was the first thing I saw after we were free.

While we were waiting for my dad to come back and our friends to pick us up, an old lady from across the street saw us. She called us into her house. She spoke only German, so we didn't really understand her. She gave us food and let us play with toys. We waited for about two hours in her garden until our friends finally came.

After staying at our friends' house for a while, we went to a guest house. There, my dad got a job as a logger so we could get money to fly to America. The guest house gave us a room, three meals a day, and money for fruit. We also met new friends who now live only half an hour away from us.

When we got enough money together, we came to Beach, North Dakota. People in the town sponsored us—and the rest is another story.

# Different

Lianne Z. Thompson, age 16

ALL THROUGH MY LIFE, I HAVE BEEN DIFFERENT FROM OTHER people. At birth I was premature, and I was the only premature baby that my mother has ever had, so right from the start, I was different.

When I started school, I was the smallest in my class in both age and appearance. Because of this, I was picked on and bullied by the other children. They made me do their work and they ate my lunch for me.

Well, I had to leave my home, the beautiful Essequibo Coast of Guyana, and move to our capital city of Georgetown. I transferred from my old school and began attending Saint Agnes Primary School, and guess what? Yes, you guessed it. I was different because I came from the coast and I spoke Creolese, which is a form of broken English. Creolese sounds quite different from the plain English that the other children spoke, so they laughed at me. But it didn't stop there. You see, the methods of teaching on the coast were far more ancient than those used in Georgetown. This was because the schools in Georgetown were well-funded and had new textbooks and a whole lot of other things that the lesser-developed schools couldn't afford. I couldn't relate to what the instructor was teaching, so the other students laughed at me and called me stupid. All through this, I kept my feelings to myself. I didn't tell my parents, because I was scared that my parents would transfer me to another school where I would have to go through an all-too-familiar routine, and I wasn't ready to go through that all over again.

I decided to set a new pace for my life. I wanted to be one of the girls; you know, I wanted to fit in. I tried changing the way I spoke, but that didn't work, so I tried focusing on my schoolwork. All of a sudden, I had this hunger inside me to do my best, to excel. That didn't get me anywhere with becoming one of the girls, but it made me see how important it was to get an education. I was slowly, but surely, raising myself to the top of the class. I admit that I wasn't the most intelligent person in my class, but I wasn't the least intelligent person either. You see, I wasn't as skilled as they were, but I was getting by.

The time came for me to take the S.S.E.E., the Secondary Schools Entrance Examination, which is taken nationwide by all students who want to go on to high school. I scored a 546 out of 600 possible points, which enabled me to be accepted into the most recognized schools in the country. In fact, it was the third highest score in the country. Many people were surprised that I had done so well, but that didn't really bother me. All that I was concerned with was that my parents were proud of me and I had outscored all those children who had given me such a hard time. For that, I will be eternally grateful to my teachers and my parents. They supported me and made that possible.

Well, the first day of high school finally came. I was so excited I didn't know what to do with myself. But boy, was I shocked when I got there. You guessed it—I was different.

At that school, children of the richest and most influential people in Guyana attended classes. Every day, their parents drove them to school in fancy cars. They wore the most expensive clothes and shopped at the most expensive stores, while poor little me was just average. I was surprised to find that these children didn't have an ounce of knowledge in their heads and, as far as I was concerned, had no right attending this school. All they could talk about was money, money, and more money.

I knew that I was different because I remembered the struggle I had been through to earn my place at the school. I spent four years in that school and my story continues.

Last July, my family and I moved to the United States from Guyana. My first few days at school here were hectic. I was so accustomed to being on the outside—you know, not fitting in—that I didn't try to socialize with the other children. I only spoke when I was spoken to. I didn't want to speak because I was afraid of how it would sound to the other students. I was afraid that they would laugh at how I sounded. That doesn't mean that some ignorant people didn't laugh—they sure did, and it made me feel angry and hurt at the same time. One thing that I learned, though, was not to let them get under my skin, and, this time, I even told my family how I felt.

My mom said that my dad wants to transfer me to another school, but I reminded him of some words he had told me when I was little. He had told me, "Honey, no matter where you go, people are going to try to pull you down and there is nothing you can do about that! Just believe in yourself and you'll get through it." Thanks to him, I am.

# When I Came to America

*Sonia Ruano, age 15*

TWO YEARS AGO I CAME TO LIVE IN THE UNITED STATES. THE FIRST days were weird, scary, and different because of going to school, forming new habits, making different friends, and learning a new language.

The first day I went to school, I was really scared. I only saw people who didn't speak the same language that I did. I didn't have anybody—only my two sisters, but they couldn't be with me. I was really scared. I always cried. The counselor took me to my classes and assigned a person to help me, but the person went off with her friends and left me alone. I went home crying and didn't want to come the next day because I didn't want to be alone.

The United States was really different. I met a lot of relatives whom I didn't know. They treated us well. The streets and the stores were different than in my country. The parks were big and the beach was cold. The water seemed like ice. The weather was cold.

It was hard for me to make friends because I spoke a different language. Most people didn't understand me. I was scared to go to classes, to go to brunch and lunch, and to speak to teachers or other students. I felt bad because I didn't understand English or anything. Everybody felt bad for me, and they were scared to talk to me because I didn't understand anything.

After some days of going to school, I met two friends. I stayed with them. They were nice, but I thought that they helped me because they felt sorry for me. But one of them said that I didn't have to be scared because, with time, I would get used to being here.

I still try my best, and I don't like to remember the first day because I can't avoid that scary feeling. By coming to this different country, we feel new, and we always feel scared, but with time we will get used to all the changes. I have learned that I have to try to be better than being scared. I have to survive.

# DEPRESSION

# Living with Depression

*Megan Christensen, age 16*

IT STARTED ABOUT FOUR YEARS AGO. DEPRESSION. I HAD HEARD about it from my parents, friends, and teachers. I didn't know exactly what was wrong with me at that point, but I knew it was something.

I first started feeling down all of the time. My grades started slipping, and I lost the majority of my friends. I felt like I wasn't wanted anymore, like there wasn't anybody out there who actually cared about me. I wanted to end my life and get out of everybody's way. My feelings about the world and myself carried on for about two full years until I finally decided to do something about it. Maybe what I tried to do was wrong, but it was the only thing I could think of doing. I wanted out, and I wanted out right then.

It was 1994, the start of the new school year. I was in eighth grade at the time, and I was having so many problems. It first started out as school-related problems, then it became troubles with my friends and parents. October 11 was the day that my grandfather died. I had flown down to Arizona earlier with my mother to see him one last time. I loved him so much, and now I didn't have him anymore. I felt that he had left me because I did something wrong. I ended up missing about two weeks of school. I didn't ever want to go back to school again. I wanted to stay with my grandpa. I ended up having to go back to school anyway. It was hard. When I got back, my friends didn't want to talk anymore. I didn't know why, and I really didn't care. I never did find out why they ditched me, so I guess I never will know.

I let all of my problems build up inside me over the next couple of years, and I never told anybody what was bothering me. I didn't think that anybody cared.

My main passion in life is the ocean. I wanted to explore the underworld more than anything. Finally, in the summer of 1996, part of my dream came true. There was a scuba diving camp in Iowa. I figured that I would try it and get away from everything. I went to camp that summer and I had fun. But as soon as I got home, all of my problems, worries, and troubles came running back to me. They wouldn't leave me alone. One week of pleasure was all that I got, but it wasn't enough. Not only did all of my troubles stay with me throughout the entire summer, but they built up inside of me until I just couldn't take it anymore. I was going to do it. The one thing that I thought was best for me and for everybody else . . . suicide.

The first thing that came to mind was to jump. I made a plan to jump off of a particular bridge that I knew of. Everything was set and I was on my way. One problem arose; I got caught. I guess I didn't care if I got caught or not, but I was hoping I wouldn't get caught until after I had achieved my goal. That way I would be dead before anybody found out. My parents found out about my "plan" and took me to the hospital for therapy. I spent the rest of my summer in therapy being lectured about how I wasn't supposed to die yet and how I had a right to continue my "precious" life. All I could think of at that point was finding a way to get out of this world without being caught.

Therapy finally ended by the time my school year began. I was now a freshman in high school, but a freshman who still had troubles, many troubles. They lingered over my head, day and night, night and day. I felt depressed all the time. I needed to find a way out, and this time I needed a way that worked.

Nineteen ninety-seven was here, and I was still alive. Then came the dreaded month of May. I couldn't take life anymore and I was going to end it right then and there. The school day came to an end and I went right home. I saw the aspirin bottle sitting on the counter and came up with an idea. Forty-nine . . . fifty . . . and then came the floor. I passed out on the floor as the fiftieth aspirin slid down my sore throat. The next thing I remember is lying in my bed, my ears ringing loudly, and seeing my future not in this world. I guess I was dreaming, because, three days later, I was awake, sitting in school, trying to think of a reason why I was still here. No reason came to mind. What had I done wrong? Did I not swallow enough aspirin? How could this not have worked?

I ended up making it through another horrifying school year, but I had something to remind me of that day back in May. I think it was an ulcer, but the doctors didn't think so. I never did tell anybody the reason for my constant stomach pains. Maybe the doctors would have been able to tell me what was wrong if I had told them what I'd done, but I wasn't about to tell anybody that. I didn't want people to look down on me like I was an idiot for doing something so stupid. Doctors examined me for the rest of the year trying to figure out what was wrong. They never found anything. Was this a miracle? I don't know.

Another miserable summer had gone by and school was back in session. Sure, I was a big, bad tenth grader, and it was supposed to be a good year, but as I expected, it wasn't.

"Something is wrong with me," I kept saying to myself. But what? Why couldn't I figure it out? Getting away from everything sounded like the best plan to me, and that is what I did.

In October of 1997, I did what I had been wanting to do for a long time. I ran away from home. I skipped school—I didn't want to go and I wasn't going to go. I ended up calling an old friend of mine to pick me up. He drove me around for awhile and then dropped me off at Spillville. Nobody could know where I was, so I decided to run to where I couldn't be found. Ridgeway was where I ended up in a couple of hours, but it wasn't far enough. I had to go farther. Somehow, I ended up getting a ride to Cresco where one of my friends lived. He tried to get me to go back home, but I just wouldn't—I couldn't. When 12:00 A.M. rolled around I told him that I had run away from home, and then it all happened. I got into his truck, and he told me that we were going to go look for some friends of his. Then I realized that he had lied and that he was taking me home. I wouldn't let him take me, but he told me that there was no way I could stop him. I guess I showed him—I pulled out a twelve-inch long knife I had been keeping in my sweatshirt because I was going to die that day. He panicked and turned the car around. I told him that I wasn't going to go home unless I was in a coffin. What was I saying? Could I really do this to my friend? No, I couldn't, but I still had my mind set on dying. Later that morning, at about 4:30 A.M., two cops pulled up to the house where I was staying. BUSTED! I couldn't believe it. I had to go to the Cresco cop shop, and then travel to the Decorah cop shop to be picked up by my parents. I didn't know what to say to them, and they didn't know what to say to me.

More and more things began to happen during the years of 1997 and 1998. I ran away again, but the consequences were much worse this time. I got sent away to a shelter for the weekend, and I had to go to court and talk to police officers. It was a horrifying experience, one that I never want to repeat.

I have many more stories that I could share with you, but I think you have gotten the basic point. The majority of my actions are caused by what I have . . . depression. Depression is a very scary thing to have, and it is no joke. There are medications available to help you through it, but none that will cure it. This is a disease that maybe cannot be prevented, but there is help. I have been in therapy for the past eight months, plus I am now on medication.

I haven't gotten rid of my type of depression, which is called manic depression, but I have found help. The medication and the therapy are a big help in my life. They have changed me from the scared, suicidal little girl that I used to be, to the person that I deserve to be. Because of my actions and the pain that I have caused myself and others, there will still be pain inside of me—forever.

A lesson to be learned from all this is to be careful what you do to your life. Life is precious, and we have only one chance to live. If you think that you have depression, don't be scared to get help. Help is out there all around us. Don't let it go too long, or the consequences will remain with you forever.

# Alley Cat

......................................

*Joie Schubert, age 17*

CLOUDS OF DARKNESS OVER MY WHOLE WORLD, THAT IS HOW I thought for a long time. No one cared, no one loved me, no one wanted to be with me—I had no one.

Dead, but so alive. Lonely, with people all around. Quiet, but always talking.

The real bottom I hit was when I was diagnosed with depression, sitting in a mental health unit in Minnesota. This was the first time I ever heard I was "mentally ill." No way, I thought. But then I had to think about all the things that were causing this depression, so that I could get over it—and it all came back to me.

My dad died when I was only two years old, and my mom later married the guy who was with my dad when he died. Years went by before I knew who he was and what had happened. I was devastated, to say the least. The remarriage took my life on a roller-coaster ride, from all the fighting and all the fakey smiles. Both of my parents were in and out of the house all the time. My brother came to live with us when he was fifteen, and my sister and I had to adjust. It never really worked out, as far as I was concerned. All three of us learned to cope with the changes that faced us, changes that seemed to happen every day. My sister played the parental role most of my childhood, so when she moved out, I lost a lot of guidance I never even knew was there. She eventually got married and went in a good direction that made her happy.

I got into drugs and went down a path that lead me where I never thought I'd go. At the same time, though, it was a release because I didn't have to save anything anymore—the first sign of depression.

My mom ended up having an affair on my dad, and it really tore things apart, not just for my family, but for my extended family as well. This is still a difficult subject for me.

The struggles I've had in life have brought me to where I am now, and I believe they're part of a hidden message. No one came right out and told me that I needed help, but all the running that I did got me the help I needed.

I was placed in a girl's group home. At first I was really closed-minded about being there, and I held back in telling anyone exactly what was going on. I walked around smiling all the time, and to tell the truth, I don't know how I did it. Every day I was faced with owning my feelings and expressing them. I was confronted about my behaviors that were unhealthy to me and to others. It took a long time to tell anyone that "yes, I was wrong" without justifying it or making it seem okay. My chemical use and peer relationships were like one in the same; bad friends do bad things. I didn't hear any of this at the time. One day, after I had been at the group home for a few months or so, I decided to run away. I never really knew why I did that. I still don't. But when I came back I was ready to work. I finally got that last bit of rebellion out of me, and it was time to move on. I knew it, and so did everyone else.

I was becoming very close to a staff member, my primary, and she believed in me. No one in my life had ever given me the time and dedication that she did. I found myself working on goals and staying behind with her just to talk. Everything I did at the group home I did for her—in the beginning—until I finally started to believe all the things that she was telling me. She gave me the incentive to do great things and to trust more in people. I hold a lot of relationships from the home dear to me—people there let me latch onto their hearts.

I went from one extreme to another while I was in the group home, and everyone noticed it. I guess the greatest feeling of all was that people chose to take a risk on me. I gave a lot during my stay there. I worked a lot on myself; enough to be able to say that it is one of my greatest accomplishments. I chose to trust people and let them help me, and I came out on top. Now I see my strengths, my behaviors, and my downfalls, and even how others affect me, so I can learn to avoid what I was in for so long.

I am so grateful for being placed in the group home and being held accountable for all the things I did. Had I not been, I would not be the person I am today. I thank them for that, I always will. It's amazing what can happen when you reach back to people who have reached out to you.

# Maze of Sorrow

........................

*Rose, age 15*

"SOMEONE LISTENING? PLEASE TELL ME SOMEONE IS LISTENING. I'm screaming! I'm going crazy here. Crazy. I can't do this anymore. I can't do this life. I don't want to live. What do I have to live for? What? I can't do this. Does anyone care? I don't care." I screamed all this out in despair. I could feel small particles of hope being torn out of my body. I was unconscious—the loud words slipping out of my mouth had no control. I couldn't find anyone or anything in me to stop the screaming. I kept stomping around the house, no one home except my poor, confused dogs. So everything was crap to me, I was ready to go. I was done living. Something really messed up clicked inside me that night. Maybe I was just lonely, maybe I was just too sad. I don't know, but all I wanted was to die.

The kitchen was coming closer and closer into view. It was blurry, but my destination was clear. I kept walking, faster, until I was in the kitchen. There—look—knives. Easy—no. Sharpest one, I need the sharpest one. I took it off the magnet that hung over a counter and stared at it. I was still in a rage, ready for death, ready to be done. The knife was scary. I started crying. Tears of pain, tears of want, confusion, anger. I slowly pulled down my shirt to reveal part of my left breast, ready to stab. Would this be easy? Would I die? I looked at my reflection in the window to the back porch. I saw no one I knew. My face a mess, my emotions screamed out, wanting to be gone. Wanting nothing but what was on the other side of life. I slowly cut myself, realizing my skin was trying to guard my heart. My skin wouldn't let me cut through, so I cut harder. I kept on cutting. There was not much to show, except blood. Small drops of blood dripping down my skin. I kept cutting. I realized I had no fear of physical pain. It was the internal stuff that really hurt.

It all sounds scary when I look back on that unforgettable night. But it taught me something about me, my life, and my dramatic emotions. This happened in the winter. The seasons have too much of an effect on what I'm feeling. Clinically, this is called seasonal affective disorder. Depression ruled my life for about two-and-a-half years. In these past seven months or so, I've seen life through brand-new eyes.

Sometimes I can't help thinking back to those sorrowful nights of sitting alone in my room with that incredible alone feeling. All I could do was cry, whine, or write. I could only think in a stream of sadness. Nothing seemed to glow with happiness, except maybe in the summer. Alone. No one understood me, and I knew it. Anyone I tried to talk to about my depression said it was "just a teenage phase," but how could being sad about *everything* be just a teenage phase? I knew it was more than a phase, and I always knew I had a real problem with depression.

"You're overly sensitive," people told me. Or how about "Just a little melodramatic." No, I knew it was more than that, and every day I knew even more how alone I was. I still know now, looking back, that it was no teenage phase, and I still know I was alone. Alone, because I wouldn't let anyone in, even if they tried. I dwelled on everything. Nothing even slightly good could come into my life, because I pushed everything away. Then I'd cry about the loss of a smile.

I can smile for real now. I feel content, even when I feel alone. It is winter, and yes, I am still struggling through the cold feelings. I've learned. It took me awhile, but I do see what life is for now. A year ago, all I wanted was death. Now my love comes from life. I've learned it's okay to be sad, but I've also learned how to stay all right through hard times. Many philosophies have helped me with this new outlook. More than philosophies, though, I know I helped myself, and that makes me proud.

In these past seven months or so, I've come to this conclusion: We are all put here to live life to its fullest. No one was put here to be stuck in gray clouds. These are words to live by. Now, I love life and all the shit that comes with it. Even the bad parts can be looked at as more experience to guide you through each day. I can always think to myself that if today sucks, maybe tomorrow I'll smile.

# MOVING

# Life Isn't Always
# As Bad As It Seems

............................................

*Leslie Chen, age 14*

SO FAR IN THE FOURTEEN YEARS OF MY LIFE, I HAVEN'T HAD TO suffer through any major problems; the only difficult situation in my life was moving. Because of my father's job, my family and I had to move overseas and back to the United States four times. It's hard to leave everything behind and go to a new and foreign place where everything seems so different from what you are used to.

When I first learned that we were moving to Hong Kong two years ago, I was devastated. I was born in Michigan and had lived there for a total of eight-and-a-half years. We had moved before, but I didn't remember much because I was too young to understand at the time. I loved everything about Troy, Michigan. The snow, the lifestyle, the people—everything. I was upset because I had to leave my friends, our church and house, and my school. At first, I couldn't imagine what it'd be like living in a place where the language was different, where I didn't know anybody. When I actually moved to Hong Kong, I felt like I didn't belong anywhere. I didn't know any of the neighbors, and it took a while to adjust to living in an apartment instead of a house. I was even more nervous about starting school. When I first visited, the building seemed bigger than the school I went to before, and everything seemed so confusing.

I was lucky when I went to school that first day, because my teacher assigned me to a "buddy." We became good friends; she ate lunch with me and introduced me to her friends, so I never felt lonely or left out. My "buddy" also took me around the school so I wouldn't get lost. Pretty soon, things became a lot less confusing and I started enjoying school. We turned out to be best friends the two years I went to that school. After a month, I began to like Hong Kong. I kept in touch with my friends from Michigan by writing letters, sending packages at birthdays and Christmas, and talking on the phone once in a while. We met many of our neighbors and found a new church. I thought that life was great.

After two years, my dad was transferred back to Michigan. It came as a surprise, because I had been told that we'd be living in Hong Kong for at least three years. I was both happy and upset at the same time. Happy because we were moving back to our old house and I would go to high school with the people I had been in sixth grade with, so I would be with my friends again. Upset because I would have to leave the friends I had made in Hong Kong. In the two years I was there, I discovered that Hong Kong was actually an interesting place. Since I am Chinese, I was able to understand some of the language in Hong Kong, and the culture there was unique. Overall, though, I was excited about going back home.

From my experience with moving, I learned that sometimes things may seem really bad when you look at them at first, but if you keep a positive attitude and try new things, it won't turn out as bad as you expect. I'm lucky to have experienced living overseas, and it's something I should be proud of. I'm also lucky because I have friends in different countries. I've realized, too, that I am better off than many other people because I haven't had to move around a lot.

Someday I may actually have to deal with a difficult situation, but I'll try to remember to always look on the bright side—and that life isn't always as bad as it seems.

# My Way Home

*Beth Jones, age 13*

I GREW UP IN A FAIRLY SMALL TOWN. I HAD CLOSE FRIENDS, WAS getting a good education, and received recognition for my efforts. It was safe to be out past dark in that town. Teenagers could walk into a store without the owner's eyes following them like they were some kind of criminal. Not one of the kids in the neighborhood ever talked about drugs or alcohol. Everyone lived without fear of violence. I lived in a dream world. I thought that every other place on earth was just as perfect. I never could have known how wrong I was.

After I finished third grade, my family moved to a place that was 150 miles from everything that I had known and loved. A place where I had no friends and where I didn't belong.

When I started school, everyone was very nice to me and I thought I would make lots of friends in no time. It took me a long time to see that they were just pretending to be my friends. They already had their cliques, and they weren't looking for new members.

I was alone again. I crawled into an antisocial hole and couldn't come back out. I didn't make any real friends and I didn't meet boys. I guess that was when I did most of my growing up. I had to be mature just to get through the pain.

My parents didn't see the side of me that showed when I was away from home. All they saw was their little girl. They still treated me like I was six years old. I tried to take on more responsibility to show them that I was old enough to handle it. In fifth grade I became editor-in-chief of the school paper that I and one of the girls in my class had started the previous year. I became involved in several activities that I didn't really want to be a part of. It got to be more than I could handle.

My parents still thought of me as a little girl. In their opinion, I was too young for everything. They never said that, but I kind of got that idea from the way they answered my questions. I was sick of hearing "Too young to date," "Too young to have a boyfriend," "Too young to go to the store alone," "Too young." Eventually, I just stopped asking.

I was also having trouble in school. My grades weren't bad or anything. I usually got As and Bs. But before I moved, I had gotten straight As. I was frustrated with my new teachers. They seemed to think that all they had to do was teach us what was in the books. The teachers in my old school taught me an additional skill. They taught me how to learn. They made me want to search for information on topics I wanted to learn about. In my new school the teachers limited what I could write about in reports and stories. They gave me topics to write about, topics I didn't even care about. That was when I knew I would have to challenge myself to learn. I still continue to do that. It's the only way I'm happy.

As for my antisocial hole, I found my way out. I'm in a clique that began when I started middle school. I found a lot of people willing to be my friends. We call ourselves "the Circle," and we're all very close. I have a boyfriend, too, although I'm not allowed to go on a date with him except to the closely chaperoned school dances. He's okay with that, though.

I'm still searching for my way home. First I have to find out what my idea of home is. All I know is that the move helped me see what the real world is like. It wasn't something that I wanted to see, but I had to in order to know that there was a world beyond my little town. I will be home some day, I know it. And I won't doubt that I'll be ready for it.

# Moving On

........................................

*Rebekah, age 18*

SOMETIMES I LOOK BACK AND I CAN'T BELIEVE HOW MUCH I HAVE changed, grown, and learned. I have had anything but a normal past, but I wouldn't change it if I could, because it has made me who I am today.

I live in Minnesota. I am a senior in high school. I am on Danceline, and I love it more than anything. This has been a busy year for me. It's like reality has slapped me in the face, but I have gained the maturity to handle it (not easily I might add). I am going on my second year here. Before this, I lived in California for five years, and that was the longest time I had ever spent in one place.

Until the age of eleven I traveled the world: a year in Spain, three in Israel, and several months each in the Canary Islands, France, Belize, Mexico, and more. Whenever people hear this, the first thing that comes to their mind is, "Are your parents rich?" Much to the contrary. I have begged for food, slept on hard benches in the rain, and spent many nights cold and hungry.

It was not always like this. I have lived in many states in the United States, too: New Mexico, Arizona, Oregon, Washington, New York, Montana, Colorado . . . anyway, you get the idea. My parents were, and in many ways still are, hippies. They would open their houses to the homeless and give food to the hungry. Their intentions were good. They were searching for God and something more than what modern American society has to offer. This is the simplest way I can explain their justifications for all we went through. This search is what led them across the world, with me tagging along.

I do not feel I was neglected or deprived. I have seen things many people don't see in a lifetime. I have met some of the most beautiful people this world has to offer, and I have experienced what many only dream of.

One day this all came to an end and I found myself living in California with my mother. A whole new phase in my life began. I had spent a couple brief years in school, but I was mostly taught at home. Suddenly I was shoved into a typical school as a fourth grader, but I had no trouble adapting. This is one of the traits I had gained over our years of travel. I began doing the normal things kids my age did, things like dressing up and playing with Barbies. But as I grew older, my priorities took the wrong path.

During my freshman year in high school, I began using drugs and concentrating only on my social life. My mother and I would have the most horrible fights. I was constantly letting her down. The only thing I really cared about was partying.

In the middle of my sophomore year, my mother couldn't stand it any longer. We were barely ever on speaking terms unless we were screaming at each other, and she could not control me anymore. She had often threatened that she would send me to live with my father, but I never took her seriously. This time she meant it. I begged her not to. I told her how I would change, that I would listen to her. She wouldn't budge. She thought I would be better off living with my father. She had my best interests in mind.

I cannot explain how this flipped my world upside down. I was leaving my family for a family I didn't even know. I was leaving the friends who were, and still are, so close to me. But the worst thing was the thought of living in a huge, freezing city. From the time we are born it is understood that we are alone, but I think there is a certain time in your life when you not only know this, but you feel it. Let me tell you, this was not an easy thing for me to accept.

After arriving in Minnesota, I went to school every day and came home. This was the extent of my life. I was lonely and depressed. I had so much free time on my hands that it was very easy for me to sit and dwell on my problems. Finally, I could take it no longer. I had to find something to occupy my time. I got a job, and in the beginning of my junior year I joined Danceline. I have stuck with both. In fact, I plan to either minor or major in dance. (I am also very interested in secondary education.)

I often wondered what it was about living with my father that helped me to mature. I came to the conclusion that my father has higher expectations of me. This helped me to set higher goals for myself and to accomplish them. One important thing I have learned is that by setting my standards high, I have a greater respect for myself and am able to respect others more.

Keeping myself busy not only took my mind off things, but helped me meet many new wonderful people. I am so much more confident in myself than I was two years ago. I am not only physically fit, but mentally, too. I took a bad situation and used it to improve myself and better my life. I have also learned a lot about the person I am. I am now able to reflect on all the wonderful things my travel and hardships have offered me. I see things with a more open perspective. This is something I value in myself, and I've found that others value this in me as well.

# In Constant Motion

*JLM, age 17*

THROUGHOUT MY LIFE I HAVE HAD TO GO THROUGH NUMEROUS moves. Moving is easier for some children than for others. When I think of kids that have to move around numerous times, the first word that usually comes to mind is "outgoing." They are used to meeting new people, right?

This was not my personality at all. I found it more difficult to meet people than most. Now don't get me wrong, if someone came up and talked to me, I'd become a whole new person. It wasn't that I was scared to talk to people, it was just that I was afraid to approach them first. And how can you expect to meet people without going out of your way to talk to them?

The first time I moved was when I was seven years old. I was moving from Oklahoma to Texas. I loved my new house and the area in which we lived. This was by far my easiest move. Second graders do not have their friends set yet. They are open to anybody and everybody.

It was not long (two years to be exact) before we moved back to Oklahoma. I was moving to a different school and town than I had lived in before. It was more difficult for me to meet new people, but it did not take long for me to fit right in. By the end of the year, I had been voted homecoming queen of the fourth grade. Everything had worked out great.

Four years later, we moved back to Texas. I was in eighth grade and going to a bigger school than I had ever attended. I was horrified. The first few days were incredibly difficult. As days went by, I began to make new friends, although everything was still not going as well as I had wanted. I had numerous friends, but none to confide in or share my problems. I would go home almost every day and cry. I mourned the loss of my old friends and confidants.

When I got to high school, however, I joined clubs and played on the varsity tennis team. I fit in great. I now had my own group of friends. We were all like brothers and sisters. I swore I would never move again. My parents talked of moving back to Oklahoma, but I said the only way we could possibly move was if we did it before my freshman year was over. My ninth grade year ended, and I thought I would get to complete my high school career at one school.

Those plans came to a sudden halt when we moved back to Oklahoma at the start of my junior year. It was only by the grace of God that some girls came and introduced themselves to me on the first day of school. We are still great friends to this day. I am now in my senior year and merely have my next move—to college—to look forward to.

College will be a different experience than my other moves. In a sense it will be easier because there will be hundreds of new people. Everyone will be searching for new friends. But I will also be all alone this time. In the past, I had the support of my family to help me through. They would encourage me every day as I arrived home from school. College will definitely be a new and exciting challenge.

I believe the older a person gets, the more difficult it is for them to move. Moving was tortuous for me, but it was a great learning experience. I have learned to be considerate of other new people and what they are going through when they come to a new area. I have been in their place before and know how good it feels when people come up and introduce themselves. When I go up to someone, it helps him or her to know that there is at least one person to talk to, and it helps me to know that I am helping someone else. I enjoy helping people, and this is one area that I can relate to.

Moving should not be thought of as a bad thing, but as a time to learn and meet new people. It seems as if I have been "in constant motion" these seventeen years, but I do not regret a single move that we have made. I have made great friends and have gotten to see and do many things.

# DIFFICULT CHOICES

# Walking Away

........................

*Dori, age 17*

I NEVER UNDERSTOOD HOW SOMETHING THAT SEEMED SO PERFECT and right in the beginning could turn out to be such a nightmare. This is what happened to my relationship with Ken. He still tries to creep into my life, but I have learned my lessons the hard way.

I met Ken in September of 1996, and he became a major part of my life. He seemed so sweet and innocent, but innocent he was not, for he turned my life into ruins. I fell in love with Ken, but all it got me was heartache and trouble. Little did I know that Ken was using a drug that controlled his mind and actions—crack. He hid it well from me.

I first became aware of Ken's drug use when we were washing our cars at the car wash. A state trooper pulled in and had a warrant to search both our cars. Luckily, he found nothing in Ken's car because I could have gone to jail, too. I felt so stupid. I finally realized why he never had money even though he had a job, and why certain weird things had happened. I told Ken that I could not and would not stay with him as long as he was using this or any other drug.

Ken followed me for months because he would not accept the fact that I would not go back to him.

I have moved on with my life now and sometimes I get more bits and pieces of the story. I found out that Ken cheated on me and took money from me. It is still hard some days, because I really did love him and he hurt me. He still calls and comes to my house, but I cannot risk talking to him. I am scared that he will sweet-talk me into going back to him.

Anyone can walk away from a bad situation, even if they love the person involved. They just have to be brave and believe that they deserve so much more. I am proof of that! I am stronger than I have ever been before. Walking away made me so!

# My Life

..............................................

*Danny Young, age 15*

WHEN I WAS TWELVE YEARS OLD, I CAME TO THE UNITED STATES to live with my mom and my stepfather. I wasn't afraid of anything when I came here. I thought living in this country would be fun and exciting. But after a while, living here seemed to be like living in any other place. I started by going to a middle school as a seventh grader. I didn't know a lot of English. On my first day of school, I met a lot of friends. I can't think of anybody who made fun of me because of how I looked or because of my accent. I think I am a very lucky person because I hear that a lot of people who emigrate from another country often don't get along with the people in their new country.

Before I came to the United States, I lived in Berlin, Germany, for more than eight years. I can speak, write, and read German fluently. I really liked it there, but my mom didn't live in Germany. I moved here because I wanted to be with my mom. I had a lot of friends over there—close friends, I mean. Most of my friends tried to stop me from coming here, but I thought that my family was more important. It didn't take me a long time to decide whether or not I wanted to come here. Many of my friends were sad, and so was my aunt. She was the one who took care of me when I was sick or in trouble or having other difficulties. I never thought that I would leave my aunt by herself, but I really wanted to see my mom. Sometimes I think I shouldn't have come here. I didn't really think about it too much, because, as I told you, living here is the same as living anywhere else.

I was born in Bangkok, Thailand. I don't really know a lot about Thailand because I moved to Germany when I was four years old. I can speak Thai, but I can't write or read it. My father told me to go to a Thai school. I also have a sister in Thailand. She is eleven years old now, and she is in the sixth grade. I haven't seen my sister for more than five years. I think a lot about her and we also talk a lot on the phone. Every time I talk to her she asks me when I'm going to visit, which makes me sad a lot of the time.

I still don't know why my mom and my dad are divorced, but I think that's probably why I had to go to Germany. I haven't asked my mom yet why she sent me to my aunt. I haven't asked her because I don't want to bring up a bad memory. I'm not mad at my mom or my dad for sending me to Germany. In fact, I enjoyed living there. I wish my mom and my dad would still love each other like they did before.

In my life, I have never faced a situation that I couldn't handle. I am a truthful person. I don't like to lie to people, and I don't like saying bad things behind anybody's back. If I have something to say, I tell that person face-to-face or I keep it to myself. I don't like making jokes about my friends because I don't like them making fun of me. I think that everybody in the world is the same, and I don't judge people by the color of their skin. I'm a person who likes to talk about relationship problems with my girlfriend.

I don't like a lot of sports. The few sports I like are table tennis, tennis, volleyball, and soccer. I have been playing table tennis for more than six years and I am really good at it. Some of my other hobbies are drawing, watching TV, talking on the phone, and shopping.

When I think about my life, I think that my life is very complicated. I also think that everybody in the world has problems, and mine can be fixed. Right now, the only goal I have is to finish high school and then go to a nice university and perhaps become an engineer. I don't know for sure yet, because after a while I might lose interest in that profession. I think that everybody should wait to see what they want to be.

It takes courage to push yourself to places you have never been before, to test your limits, to break barriers. And for me, the day came when the risk it took to remain tight inside the bud was more painful than the risk it took to blossom.

# Changing Schools

......................................................

*Melina Domec, age 17*

A DIFFICULT SITUATION IN MY LIFE AROSE LAST NOVEMBER WHEN I was approached about switching schools. I had attended a private school all my life, and it was difficult having to choose what to do.

From kindergarten through twelfth grade, I grew up with the same surroundings and people every day. I grew accustomed to the regulations and began to accept their imperfections. In high school, I broadened my horizons by getting involved with student council and other school activities. It didn't take long for me to become attached to every minor detail of this small school. My senior year started off with a bang! I was a cheerleader and played both basketball and volleyball. I went to every school function and unexpectedly became homecoming queen in October.

When November rolled around, however, my parents confronted me about switching schools. They wanted me to get a scholarship so I could go to college. Going to a public high school was the only way I could attain this particular scholarship, because my private high school was not accredited. This was the hardest decision I'd ever had to make. I would be leaving all my friends and everything I had accomplished in all those years. On the other hand, I would be helping my parents save money, which is what I knew I needed to do. I knew that there would be difficult decisions to make concerning my future, but I never expected them to arrive so soon. This was only one of the many decisions I would have to make in my lifetime, so I decided I might as well make the right one. All my life I had wanted to graduate from a public high school; now I would be getting my wish, but it would be unhappily obtained.

The particular scholarship I was applying for would allow me to go to college tuition-free. My parents always believed that my sisters and I would be rewarded for our good grades by getting a scholarship, which is what should follow long years of hard work and determination. My mother had been working on finding out every detail about this scholarship before even mentioning it to me because she wanted to be sure that she was doing the right thing. I could tell this was an intense issue for my parents as well—my mother's sister was the assistant principal of the school I was leaving. But she wasn't the only relative I had there. My mother's other sister, one brother, and a brother-in-law all worked for the school—not to mention my mother herself. Obviously my parents loved the school and would never dream of taking me out unless an opportunity arose that they could not resist. My parents and I faced a lot of bitterness and heartache from our loved ones as we made a decision they did not approve of. However, after all was resolved, we put our worries aside and decided to go with our hearts' desire.

After a long struggle, I decided to give public school a chance. Besides, I wouldn't have to wear uniforms anymore, and I would probably make new friends to help me through each day. The starting date was January 12, 1998 (the beginning of the second semester).

My first day of school was hectic. I had a few problems finding my classes because there were so many people and buildings! But after a few days everything seemed routine, and I was beginning to enjoy this "new life" that would have to end in May.

If anyone were to ask me if I had made the right decision, I would have to say yes. Not only did I get my wish of graduating from a public high school, but I answered my parents' wishes by earning a scholarship. However, if I could advise anyone, I would say to start at the beginning of the year. It would be easier to learn where all the buildings are if somebody else were learning it with you!

# RELATIONSHIPS

# Waiting Is Okay

..............................

*Cieltia, age 17*

"HOW MANY BOYS HAVE YOU BEEN WITH?" KEVIN ASKED ME.

"What do you mean by that?" I asked him.

"You know what I mean. How many boys have you had sex with?"

I could have lied to him, but I told him the absolute truth. "To be completely honest, I have never had sex with a boy before."

"What!?!" he screamed at me. "You mean to tell me that you are a seventeen-year-old virgin?" He thought for a moment and said, "Are you serious?"

"Yes," I told him. "I wouldn't joke about something like that." Since we were on the phone together and the silence between us was so overwhelming, we both hung up.

I couldn't believe how upset Kevin had been. He was supposed to be my boyfriend. How could the person who claimed to love me not understand that I was a virgin? We had only been going out for about a month, and the subject of sex never came up. I knew that it was bound to come up one day, but I wasn't prepared to talk about it.

Two days later, Kevin decided to call me back. He was ready to talk this time.

"I'm sorry for the way I acted the other night," Kevin confided. "You really surprised me."

"I know that I shocked you, but you had a right to know," I said.

"Why are you waiting?" Kevin wanted to know.

I thought for a little while and said, "I guess I'm waiting to find that special person to give myself to."

"I understand that," said Kevin. "To tell you the truth, I wish that I was still a virgin. Are you going to wait until you get married?"

"You know, I probably will," I answered. "Why should I rush myself when I'm not ready?"

"I should have taken my time. I lost my virginity at the age of fifteen. I'm now nineteen, but I wish I would have waited."

"I don't want you to think that we'll have sex. Don't get your hopes up," I told him.

"That wasn't even on my mind. I'm not all about having sex. I respect the fact that you want to wait."

"I just don't want you to keep hoping that I'll change my mind anytime soon," I said. "Sex, to me, is very precious."

"I know that. I just don't understand how you can wait for such a long time," he added.

"I'll admit, it does take a lot of patience and self-control. I just have to be strong. I'm not a dog, I am able to control myself."

"You are an amazing girl, do you know that?" Kevin asked me.

"I'm starting to think that I am," I admitted. "I want people to respect me, not ridicule me."

"Trust me, I do respect you and your beliefs," Kevin confessed.

Kevin and I talked on the phone for a while longer, and then we hung up. Our conversation made me think a lot. At first, Kevin made me feel ashamed for being a virgin. Then I realized that I have nothing to be ashamed of. I should be very proud of myself for waiting so long to have sex.

Not having sex has been my own decision. My mother has instilled values in me that I cannot overlook. I know that I am not ready to accept the consequences of my actions. If I became pregnant, how would I take care of a baby? I can barely take care of myself, let alone a small baby. If I contracted a sexually transmitted disease, how would I be able to live with myself? I would be miserable for the rest of my life.

People ask me all the time if I've ever wanted to have sex. I tell them of course I've wanted to, but I practice self-control. I have had opportunities, but it's all about self-respect. I respect my body too much. I want to keep my innocence for as long as I can.

I feel that when it's the right time for me, I'll know. I am a seventeen-year old virgin, and I know that waiting is okay.

# Friendship

......................................................

*Christine Davis, age 14*


A DESIRE OF MY LIFE HAS ALWAYS BEEN TO HAVE A BEST FRIEND MY own age. Ralph Waldo Emerson once said, "We walk alone in the world. Friends, such as we desire, are dreams and fables." As a four-teen-year-old home-schooled child, I have also had that dream. During these past ten years of home schooling, I have not known many girls my own age.

Activities have often substituted for this lack of a best friend. Activities that are related to music bring a special joy into my life. My days are filled with piano and harp practice. I enjoy playing for my family. Singing is another way I express my feelings. I take voice lessons with my little brother. Learning new songs together, we often forget the time.

The relationships I enjoy with my family are important. Family vacations provide good opportunities to grow in family unity. For my brother's birthday last summer, we camped by the Root River in southern Minnesota. We enjoyed a leisurely canoe trip down the scenic Root River.

Agate hunting on Lake Superior is another favorite vacation. We go in the spring after the snow melts to find the best agates. My brothers and I compete for the best agate collection. The competition gets intense.

On Saturdays, when most children play with their best friend, my family and I play games such as hearts, canasta, whist, Risk, and so on. We also play baseball in the nearby park with my dad as the pitcher.

Because I do not have a girlfriend to play with, I often play with my brothers. We dress up in Dad's old army uniforms and camouflage our faces. We climb the big tree in our front yard to spy on passersby.

My family and I often go to my grandparent's house by Swan Lake. We catch the most delicious walleye. In the winter, when the lake is thick enough, we go ice fishing with my cousin. Snapping turtles, the size of a tire, sometimes appear. The road is often covered with frogs, so my brothers and I have frog catching contests. Again, the competition is intense!

My mother is a great help to me in school. For example, I decided to learn Hebrew as a second language. My mother worked with me and we went to the classes together. We studied together before each class, just like best friends.

We share our home with four cats. My kitten may not be a best friend, but she always wants to be with me. Her frolicking and playing can entertain me for hours. Along with our other three cats, she keeps our home full of activity.

Since I do not have a special girlfriend my own age, I have devoted my time to academic studies. I study hard because I will attend college soon. I spend much time reading books, and I love writing book reports. I probably read about one hundred books a year.

In addition, I enjoy gardening with my mom in our backyard. We have made four beautifully landscaped ponds there. It is a special place to retreat to when I seek solitude.

If I had a best friend my own age, we could go ice skating, biking, and swimming, dress up the cats in baby clothes, or even share secrets. I would offer encouragement to her. Honesty would be important. I would try to understand her at all times, for I know to have a friend, you must be a friend.

Even though I do not have a girlfriend my own age, I enjoy being with my family and doing activities with them. I have learned many rules of friendship with my own family. Someday, God may bring a girlfriend, my own age, into my life. Until then, I will consider ways I can be a best friend to those around me, for they are God's gifts to me.

## THE WAY TO BE A FRIEND

### By Craig E. Sathoff

*The way to be a friend is just to strive each day to be,*
*A firm believer in the strength of human dignity.*
*To teach each fellow man the way that you would like to be,*
*With deep respect for each man's worth and his integrity.*
*The way to be a friend is just to keep a smiling face,*
*To realize that laughter adds a special note of grace.*
*The way to be a friend is just to give and give and give,*
*Of help and care and kindly words each day that you shall live.*
*To shun away each petty doubt and open up the heart,*
*To let in thoughts of love and trust, which is how friendships start.*

I realize I have developed many friendships within my own family. Henry Adams once said, "One friend in a lifetime is much; two are many; three are hardly possible."

# SELF-ESTEEM AND OTHER
# NEW PERSPECTIVES

# Life's Little Lesson

......................................

*Shelley, age 17*

I STARED IN DISBELIEF AT THE RESEARCH ASSIGNMENT HANDED down by the teacher. It is only the second week of school! After the initial shock, I noticed that the paper wasn't due until the end of September. Whew! I shoved the assignment into my backpack; I'll worry about it later.

"Later" turned out to be the final weekend before the assignment was due. After digging into my bag for what seemed to be an eternity, I found the thin sheet of torment. "Write about the primary and secondary succession of a pond or temperate deciduous forest in Michigan." What? Undaunted, I decided to check the Internet. Feeling nothing could go wrong with my plan, I arrived at the library. After patiently waiting for the computer to log on, I combed through the entire 100-some "relevant" items Netscape came up with. Not one of them proved useful. By the old-fashioned method, I found almost all the ecology books in the library. Several hours of ecological book search yielded nothing of value either. My head started to swirl. Just as I was about to faint, I remembered the metro-parks. Didn't the teacher say the Nature Center at Stony Creek explains everything regarding succession? My mind cleared right up. I'll just go over there tomorrow and get the information I need. Procrastination shall not beat me yet!

The next day, my parents and I embarked on the twenty-minute drive to the center. I had imagined going to a museum-like building. Instead, the ranger there handed me a map and pointed out the trail I was to take to get the information. Always eager for adventure, we decided to take the hike. As we started down the landscaped trail, little did I know that I was advancing on a journey that would forever change my perspective on life.

The September day was unusually sunny and warm for Michigan. Along with the birds' constant chirping, butterflies and grasshoppers danced in front of us, welcoming us deeper into nature, their home. My mind began to be cleared of impending worries and started to fly with the little creatures. Beside me, my parents joked and laughed as if they were kids again. We raced up and down the hills and tried to summon the names of different dragonflies we once knew so well. I hadn't bonded with my parents in such a profound way in years. The sun seemed to shine extra bright as we walked on. Our joy echoed back from the surrounding forest. Everything was in perfect harmony.

As the two-mile journey drew near an end, I lingered behind a little bit. Seeing my parents walk hand in hand under the shades of waving trees, I suddenly realized my newfound knowledge of life. True happiness, I perceived, is obtained not through what we get physically, but through what we become spiritually. To live life fully is to make the best effort to reach all dreams, absurd though some may be, and to not regret later on for not trying. This is how to succeed. Often, people get caught up in the competitiveness of the modern world. Sometimes everyone has to take a step back, relax, and be satisfied.

As our car pulled out of the gravel parking lot, a quote I read long ago jumped to mind: "You smell the salt in the air? You feel the sunlight on your skin? That's all real. You see all of us together? That's real. Life is wonderful. It's a gift to be alive, to see the sun and breathe the air."*

* Maya Lin, quoted by Jim Sexton in *USA Weekend*, reprinted in "Quotable Quotes," *Reader's Digest*, March 1997, p.49.

# Growing Pains

........................................

*CSM, age 18*

If asked to describe my behavior during my adolescent years with one word, it would have to be "dysfunctional." Although I live in a nice home with two parents who provide sufficiently for me and my two siblings, I have always felt empty and unloved. All my life I have desperately tried to please my parents, yet it seems my efforts have always been in vain. "You're stupid," or "You make me sick" were my daily compliments, and still are. My grades never met their expectations, even when I tried my hardest, and my physical features were unfavorable to them. "That's good, but next time do better," were the words I heard, but "We're proud of you," is what I longed to hear. Even when they said, "We're proud of you," it seemed absurd and preposterous because I could see the disappointment in their faces. They seemed more elated with my brother playing basketball or my younger sister's beauty than my hard-earned B+ in Algebra II. I felt worthless and angry at their callousness, yet I tried to please them in other ways.

"You need to go on a diet, Miss Piggy," was my mother's constant reminder during my early teenage years. Although I wasn't eating any more than most girls my age, my hips and thighs seemed to explode when I turned twelve. It was already painful to be teased at school by strangers, but to have someone I loved and trusted cut me down erased what little self-esteem I had left. So, I took my mother's advice and went on diets to look like her. Yet my mother is 5 feet 8 inches tall and weighs a mere 115 pounds. I had set myself up for failure. I took diet pills, laxatives, diuretics, and anything that claimed to cause weight loss. After eating, I would pretend to use the bathroom and, instead, force what little I had eaten back up through my esophagus into the "porcelain god." This habit contin-ued for almost two years before my parents confronted me about my sickness. My mother apologized for making me feel the way I did and has since stopped calling me names. Still, I can see the dis-gust in her face when she looks at me. To this day I don't know which is worse, the sting from her cruelty, or the sting from the burned and torn tissue in my esophagus left from the gastric acids from vomiting.

Even though I should have learned from this incident, I didn't. I thought by making better grades the following school year, my par-ents would forgive me for what I had done as a sophomore. My goal was to make all As, even if it meant staying up all night studying, but fate ruled and I kept making Bs in math. Again I had failed and therefore had to readjust. To win their approval, I resorted to help-ing out around the house by dusting or folding clothes without being reminded to do so. Still, things were not working. I was con-stantly being fussed at, and half the time I did not know why. When my mother came home from work, she would fuss at me because I hadn't asked her if I could wash the clothes, regardless of the fact that I was trying to be helpful.

It appeared they were out to get me and make me miserable. Sometimes, when conversing on the phone with one of my friends, I would find my mother eavesdropping on my conversa-tions and later questioning to whom I was talking and why. And when they were displeased or angry at me for something small or minor, such as arching my eyebrows or wanting to have a friend sleep over, my parents would bring up past mishaps to make me feel doltish and worthless.

With all this anxiety and these mixed emotions bubbling inside, I did something I now will regret for the rest of my life. I started drinking and, to make a long story short, I went to school drunk. That incident was a catalyst, setting off a chain of unwanted reac-tions. Even though I had never before gotten in trouble at school, I was now recommended for expulsion. No longer were student council, track, renaissance, and honor society part of my goals for my senior year. Dreams and aspirations I had been working toward were stripped away from me with the blink of an eye. I felt as though my world was crumbling before my eyes. I had not only let my parents, grandmother, and teachers down, but I had let myself down. I suddenly became fearful of my future, for I had to deal with the fact that after years of watching our family deteriorate because of my father's drinking, I was beginning to walk in his footsteps.

Those two weeks of not going to school hurt my grades badly and left me in a state of depression. My parents were angry for a long time. They kept asking, "Why did you do this to us? Don't you think people will talk about us?" From these selfish statements I grew bitter—they were not worried about my future, but their own. My life was a living hell in the months that followed. When I finally returned to school, students snickered behind my back and teachers shook their heads as I passed them in the halls. So much for being perfect.

During that period, my life hit rock bottom. Failure, loneliness, and self-hatred prevailed in me for a long time. Suicide seemed my only escape, but the thought of breaking my grandmother's heart was, and sometimes still is, the only thing that kept me going. Sensing my loneliness, she told me, "Parents say things they don't mean, but just hang on and everything will be all right, because we all make mistakes." She also pointed out how blessed I was to have parents who kept me "well groomed and provided for." Immediately afterwards, my grandmother secretly slipped five dollars into my pocket and told me, "I love you, so don't go breaking my heart." Although she couldn't afford to buy me the $50 pair of jeans like my parents, she made me feel special and that I had a purpose.

I am proud to say that I am now a senior and have survived the growing pains! Community organizations outside of school have filled the void in my weekly schedule—and in my heart. The

Assumption Youth Group has comfortably taken the place of track and field. Through my difficulties, my friends and church parishioners prayed with me, and I truly believe that without them and the Lord, I would not be able to tell my story. Through prayer, I found a strength within myself I had no idea existed! Sarcastic remarks from my parents no longer sustain their potent venom. I have grown partially immune to them and have learned to not let cruel or ignorant remarks dampen my mood. Instead of seeking revenge, or being resentful, I pray and ask the Lord for guidance.

I have finally outgrown my dysfunctionalities with the help of love, experience, and time. Accepting that I am only human and entitled to a few faults and mistakes has helped me enjoy life more than before. When I do my best I am satisfied with my accomplishments, even when they fall short of my parents' expectations, because I love myself. I no longer fool around with diet pills or chemicals that harm instead of help the body. From first-hand encounters with drugs and alcohol, I now know that they do not help no matter what the situation may be. Dealing with problems soberly is the only way I will solve them. I may not be Cindy Crawford with Einstein's IQ, but I'm happy. Life is not always about pleasing others. Most times, life is about doing what one feels is right. Looking for satisfaction in other people's eyes only results in frustration; we must all find contentment within ourselves.

# The Permanent Reminder
# of Success

..................................

*J. McD, age 15*

IT ALL STARTED ABOUT FIVE YEARS AGO. I WAS TEN YEARS OLD, and I had dreamed of being a pitcher, just like my older sister. I was in my backyard with my dad, and it was my first real pitching lesson. I was so excited, it felt like my heart was going to pop out of my chest. I was going to be just like my older sister, whom I admire. This was a big day for me, but it didn't turn out like I planned. I thought I was going to go out there and blow my dad away because I was so good. I thought I was going to be the Nolan Ryan of softball. The first day of my pitching career was the worst. After that first day, I just wanted to go inside and cry and forget about softball altogether. My dad ended up convincing me to go back out and try it again the next weekend. We worked really hard, and I could feel myself improving. Each weekend my dad and I would go out and work on my pitching. And every weekend I would improve a little more and get a little more excited about pitching.

My first season of softball came and went. It was a discouraging year. Our team was 3 and 10, and I probably pitched about twelve of the sixty-five innings we played. The next year I wanted nothing to do with pitching. I thought I was horrible and I wanted nothing at all to do with the sport. My dad encouraged me to keep trying. The next season, I got about as much pitching time as I did the first year, but I ended being a really good catcher.

I worked on my pitching in the off-season, and I wasn't nearly as discouraged as I was the first year. I was determined to get better.

My dad and I worked during all my free time. The next season was much more successful. I ended up getting about the same amount of pitching time as the other two pitchers. It showed me that I wasn't a bad pitcher, I just needed to work harder than the other two pitchers and be more committed. So, during the next off-season, you could bet that my dad and I worked on my pitching every chance we could get. It was great to feel equal to the other two pitchers, and I was determined to become better than them. The next season was a huge success; for the first time, our team had more wins than losses. We had gone 63 and 42 with one tie. This was a big year for our team. Not only did we have more wins than losses, but we were only one game from going to Nationals. Unfortunately, we didn't make it. (Nationals is the highest you can go, it's like the World Series of softball.) Our goal for the next year was to go to Nationals and finish among the top thirty teams.

That next year we were going to have the advantage. We were in the under-fourteen division, with eleven of the twelve of us turning fourteen that season, and as thirteen-year-olds we had almost qualified to go to Nationals. As you can imagine, we were all very excited. This season I was especially determined to be the best pitcher on the team. My dad and I practiced all the time. We worked on some new pitches, and I worked on getting stronger when I wasn't practicing. This was going to be the best season of my young career.

Finally, summer rolled around. Our first tournament wasn't what I expected at all. We lost our first three games, and we were fighting for second-to-last place. I think that we were so sure of ourselves that we got overconfident. The next tournament was a success. We took second place, and I got to pitch three of the five games. We won the three games I pitched. It was a great feeling to win those three games. I felt like I was getting the respect I deserved for being a good pitcher. The season was going great—we were 96 and 6. We had lost only three games since our first tournament and we qualified for Nationals. We were going to Oregon! We had worked for this all year, and finally it paid off.

When we got to the field, I felt like a little kid in a candy store. Everything seemed so big and exciting. It was our first game and we were all nervous. I felt like I was going to throw up I was so nervous. Once the game started, all that disappeared. After the first pitch, I felt like it was just me and the catcher on the field. I was throwing strike after strike, going through batters like gamblers go through money. It was a great feeling. I was in a zone; no one could stop me. That was my first perfect game and I chose a great time to have it. After we won our first game against the Wheat Ridge Mirage of Colorado, we all went out and celebrated. We went to bed early that night anticipating, what tomorrow would bring us.

The next day was just as great as the first. We had four games with our first game starting at 7:30 A.M. and our last game ending at 10:30 P.M. We won all four games. We were very excited about our wins, but we were tired from playing four games in 100-degree weather. I had thrown three games and I was still on fire. It was the greatest feeling in my life—except I broke my finger on my pitching hand during the first game while diving for a ball. I continued to play, even though I was in horrible pain.

The next day our first game was at 8:30 A.M. against the Hacienda Heights All Stars of California. This was a big game. If we won, we would be in the championships; if we lost, we would go home. I pitched my heart out, but my broken finger and lack of sleep caught up with me. I was exhausted and in pain. I pitched the whole game and we ended up losing 2 to 3. It was a devastating loss after going so far and working so hard. We ended up taking third place out of forty-five of the best teams in the country. It was a tough loss, and now I have a crooked finger. It is my permanent reminder that working hard, never giving up, and following your dreams pays off in the end.

# The Sky's the Limit

........................................

*Kerri Long, age 17*

When I was asked to join Explorers, I was a little nervous about joining a group that was mostly boys. My friend Jen and I went to a meeting and it seemed like a group that we wanted to get involved in, so we joined.

Being the only two girls was far from easy. I felt like the guys were constantly waiting for us to mess up or complain about getting our hands dirty. It got even harder when Jen decided not to come anymore. Any girl jokes the guys made were then geared toward me, and I didn't have Jen there by my side anymore. There were times when I wanted to quit because I didn't know if I could handle it anymore on my own, but I wasn't going to let them get to me, so I stuck with it.

Deciding to stay in Explorers was one of the toughest decisions I've made, but it was also one of the best. The Post has given me a new sense of self-esteem and confidence. When we're running hose drills or search-and-rescue drills, I wonder if I'm as good as they are. However, it's the feeling I get when I accomplish the task at hand that tells me I am.

I used to see myself as a burden to the Post. Now I see myself as a member who can pull her own weight and do her share of push-ups. I've had to prove to them—and to myself—that I can do it. Now they respect me as someone who can take care of herself.

Because of the Post, I have learned to face my fears head-on. When I told my leaders that I didn't want to do ladder work because of my fear of heights, they wouldn't take no for an answer. I stood at the bottom of the ladder and looked up to the top, which seemed to stretch on forever. It was because of the support of my Post that I was able to climb the ladder despite my fear. When I came back down I had the best feeling about myself because I had fought my fear. I proved to my Post and myself that even though I'm a girl, I can do anything any guy can do, if not better.

# Social Crisis

*Cassie, age 16*

FROM THE TIME I WAS SMALL AND FIRST STARTED SCHOOL I WAS told that I was ugly. So, when I became a teenager, I thought I was so ugly that I had to get up early every morning to have enough time to load my face with make-up, put my hair in a bun and tendrils, and find the trashiest clothes to wear to school. You may wonder why I did something like that. I did it because I *believed* the rude kids at school and I thought it was the only way I could attract guys.

I attracted guys all right! So many that I didn't know how to deal with it. The problem was, they were the wrong types of guys. I wanted a decent guy, but only the abusive guys wanted anything to do with me. They saw me as an "easy piece," all because of how I dressed, did my hair, and made up my face. I went from one guy to another without gaining anything but bruises and busted lips. All the guys wanted was my body, and when I wouldn't give myself to them, they beat me. For two years I was considered a "tease."

My parents never knew about the beatings. All they knew was that because of how I was dressing, I was considered a "tease" and an "easy piece." I kept making excuses about the bruises and busted lips, so they had no idea about what was going on with the guys.

I came home crying day after day, week after week, asking my parents why this was happening to me. They told me that it was because of how I was carrying and presenting myself. They also told me that if I obeyed God's Commandments it wouldn't happen as much, if at all. From that time on I was required to wear decent clothes to school. Of course, I was a very rebellious teenager. I wore decent clothes to school, but I took trashy clothes with me and changed once I got to school. I did this for two years. I am not bragging about it because I am not proud of it.

One day in seventh grade I got in trouble for cussing out a teacher and I was sent to the office. When my mother got there she almost had a heart attack when she saw how I was dressed. She talked to the teacher and principal, and got my punishment reduced from one day's suspension to one day's detention.

When we got home, my mom and dad had a long talk with me about how I was acting and dressing. I decided that I had to change my attitude, the way I dressed, and the way I carried myself. I knew that I would have to have some help, not only from my friends and family, but also from God.

That summer I started, with the help I needed, to make some changes. I started to dress like a young Christian girl should. My attitude went from angry to moderate. I toned down the make-up so you wouldn't be able to tell that I had any on. The more decent guys started coming around. Of course, I wasn't perfect, but I started to get to know the guys before I went out with them. On my dad's advice, I started making better friends, friends who, if I was called "Hey tease," would jump in and say, "Hey, her name is Cass."

That next school year I still was considered a "tease" and an "easy piece," but my few friends and I knew how I'd changed. Since 1988 I have had one decent friend who is a guy. No, he was not perfect. He got in a lot of trouble by skipping school, drinking, and doing drugs. Although he did these things, he was always there for me. He, my mom, my dad, and the few other friends I had helped me overcome a lot by their prayers and encouragement.

I still have problems with guys. I still sometimes don't think before I jump into a relationship. I've learned the hard way that I can't do this anymore because it leads back to the beatings and people not taking me seriously.

My one decent guyfriend has also changed for the better. The only way either of us could have changed so much is through God's grace, hope, and love.

To you girls out there who are labeled with or headed for the same titles that I had for two years, you are in my prayers. Believe me, trying to change your ways without God is a lot harder to accomplish than with God. If it wasn't for prayer and God's grace, I wouldn't have gone from a "tease" to a respected young Christian girl. Just turn your problems over to God. I had to learn the hard way. Can you learn the same lesson the easy way? I hope so, and God bless!

# The Long Gravel Road

........................................

*Sarah Richey, age 17*

SUMMER WAS MY FAVORITE TIME OF THE YEAR. AS A CHILD, I always waited for school to end. I loved school, but I loved the summer even more. No more schoolwork, no more early mornings, and no more beautiful days wasted by staying inside of a building. I was a tomboy when I was younger. I loved to spend my time climbing trees and putting my feet in the mud. The word "summer" brings me back to when I was a little girl going to my great-grandmother's house every Monday morning.

Turning down that long gravel road, I couldn't wait to see my cousins again. As soon as I arrived, I would go inside and kiss my great-grandmother, Maw Maw Z. She was always excited to see mother and me, but I was probably more excited than she was. I would run next door to my great aunt's house to find Sam and Erika, my two second cousins. Sam and Erika helped me make many fond memories, because they were always providing adventures for the three of us to embark upon.

A farm usually has a lot of open space—a lot of open space and a lot of things to do! I remember looking up at a huge oak tree that stood high above the ground and feeling extremely excited. I really do not know why, but I think it was because the huge oak tree contained Erika's tree house. The tree house was awesome! It had a kitchen, some chairs, plastic dishes, and many other playthings. I always looked forward to playing in the tree house, but I had a hard time climbing up the tree to get to it. I hated the obstacle of getting up the tree, but somehow I always made it.

Tree houses and cousins were not the only highlights in my summer. Outside in the open air I could relax and lose myself in my thoughts. Whether I was feeding a newborn calf or sheep, I always enjoyed what I was doing. Inside of my great-grandmother's glorious house I sometimes found myself looking around and wondering what it was like to grow up in this great house many years ago, like my grandmother did. I often asked my great-grandmother about her life before she was married. She told me stories about when she and my great-grandfather were courting. She would also share stories about her life and raising sixteen children. Listening to her stories was one of my favorite pastimes. Watching her face light up every time she mentioned her life in the "younger" years made me smile.

Perhaps all of this is why I grew up to be the way I am. Climbing the oak tree presented a struggle, but I learned to overcome it so I could reach my goal. Perhaps I am strong-willed because I learned early on that I had to overcome barriers and obstacles if I wanted to reach the top. Sometimes, when I feel like I cannot go on, I close my eyes and imagine myself as a free-spirited child again and I somehow get through the hard times.

Being out in the country taught me to appreciate everything that I have, and everything that is yet to come. My childhood was a pleasant one, and I hope that my children also will have the good fortune to lead a special childhood. My children will not have the privilege of meeting my great-grandmother, because every day she becomes weaker and she is not the strong-willed woman she once was. I was lucky to have spent many years of my life with her. Someday she will pass away, but I will always remember the memories we made, and the lessons I learned down the long gravel road.

# Sexual Assault

# Psychotic Pervert

........................................

*Anonymous, age 15*

IT SEEMS AS THOUGH EVERYTHING YOU DON'T WANT TO FORGET you can't remember, and everything you don't want to remember you can never forget. I don't remember a lot from second grade, but I'll never forget Maureen.

We had just moved into a nice house and I had recently switched schools. My parents didn't get home from work until 5:00 and I got home from school at 3:30, so I needed a baby-sitter. My mom met Maureen, who was in sixth grade and lived down the street from us. My mom thought she would be a perfect baby-sitter. She lived close to us and seemed like a nice, responsible girl. Everyday when I would come home from school, she would be waiting at my house and ready to play. I loved it. We would have a snack, then watch TV or play games. She even did my homework for me. But as time went on, something seemed kind of weird about her.

She would say and do strange things; such as look through my underwear drawer or ask me if I had ever kissed anybody. I thought it was weird at the time, but I figured, she's older than me, so maybe that's what big girls do.

One day after school, Maureen came over and asked if she could borrow one of my training bras. I wanted her to like me, so of course I said yes. The next day, she came over and started taking pictures of me. I didn't know why, because I was only seven, but I posed for the camera because she told me to. Then she did something really scary: she told me to take off my clothes.

I took off all my clothes and she just looked at me standing there stark naked in my room. As she started to move closer to me I was scared and confused. I wanted to run, but all I could do was sit there, because until 5:00, she was my mom. So I just sat there as she started to touch me.

Her hands rubbed against my face as she started to kiss me. I had never kissed anyone before, unless you count the pecks under the sand table in kindergarten. I remember silently crying out for help. I felt so hurt and used. As she was about to do more, I heard my mom walk in the door. Maureen quickly jumped up and told me to get dressed. I threw on my shirt when I heard my mom's footsteps. She walked through the door and asked Maureen what we did that day. Maureen told her we watched TV and played games. I felt like I was forced to go along with Maureen's story.

"Yeah, Mom, it was a lot of fun," I said, wishing she could hear my silent cries.

The next afternoon, things got worse. I felt like we were on a roller coaster and every time she came near me, the hills got steeper and steeper. I remember her walking into my room and telling me to take off everything except my bra. She, in turn, would take off everything except her underwear, so it would be like we were naked. I did what I was told and she took me into the bathroom. I remember laying on the ground and her kissing me. I remember her telling me that this had to be our secret, because my mom couldn't find out. So I kept it a secret that night when my mom came home. I didn't say a word. Maureen kissed me good-bye and left.

I wanted to say something. I wanted to cry and tell my mom everything. But when I tried to speak, no words came out. Maureen never came over to baby-sit anymore. I think my mom must have suspected something. I told her six years later. She wanted to take her to court, but I wouldn't let her. I thought everything was my fault. I felt like I should have said, "No! Get away from me!" But after years of thinking about it, I realized it wasn't my fault. I realized she was just a psychotic pervert who needed to molest a second grader to make herself feel better.

Maureen graduated from high school last year, but she still lives on my block. When I go by her house it reminds me of all the painful memories, but I try not to think about it. Whenever I baby-sit, I think about how disgusting it would be to confuse and hurt a child, like Maureen did to me.

# The Nightmare

*Maria G. Caballero, age 17*

IN THE SILENCE OF THE NIGHT, DOORS WERE LOCKED, LIGHTS were off. All the inmates in the Girls Ranch Detention Center were probably praying to soon be released. Closing my eyes, I also prayed that I would soon be free—like a bird in my dream. But the darkness in my eyes appeared and a nightmare began, bringing back a memory that would forever change my life.

In my dream it was a summer day, the sun as shiny as it could be. I could clearly smell the dirt and hear the animals. I could see a little girl playing in a yard, a field in the countryside of Mexico. In her laughter I could hear her happiness to be back on the land on which she was born. In her eyes I could see she was a dreamer, a flower full of life, a little girl who didn't expect to grow up in less than a minute.

Then she was inside this old brick house. I could see flashes of the whole place—one room after another. There were no doors, no windows. When she tried to run out of it, a young teenage boy blocked her way. He pushed her into one of the rooms with just a look. He seemed familiar, an older play friend. Walking backward, she knew that this was not a game like one they used to enjoy. He was betraying their friendship.

She was pressed against a corner, confused, not knowing if she could just scream, "Daddy!" and be safe. But the darkness of the room wouldn't let the words come out. The old house falling apart made the boy's voice softly echo in her ear: "You won't get hurt." A beam of light allowed her to see his eyes as her little body shook. (I could feel her pain.) His hands were all over her body—it was like a rose was getting ripped from its bush, tearing her hopes and dreams out of reality. To her, reality meant nothing. She had a body of a seven year old, but he had destroyed her innocence. Closing her eyes, she tried to block out this day forever, not knowing that one day it would haunt her, and it would haunt her forever.

When my eyes opened my body was shaking, tears falling from my eyes. I looked around the white, cold, and empty room that was mine at the Ranch and I knew I was safe. I tried to catch my breath, but my heart was beating faster by the second. I tried to explain to myself what was going on, but I didn't understand what had happened. I couldn't think. Was it just a bad dream?

Every day I would go back to that nightmare. I would see the little girl slowly dying inside. After several nights, I couldn't take it. I was getting sick.

One morning I started to shake in the breakfast room. My bones felt weaker every day. I felt cold even though I was sweating. That morning, my counselor at the Ranch asked me not to go to school with the other girls. When I sat down on one of the gray chairs, she looked at me and asked, "What's wrong?"

I said, "I don't understand myself." I told her about my nightmares.

When her eyes turned my way I could feel a cold, intense look, and then she asked, "Have you ever been raped?" That word went from my ear to my blood, from my blood to my heart. I could feel my heart in my stomach beating faster by the second. The word had shocked me. As I sat there, I cried. I realized that the little girl in the nightmare was me. I had blocked that day from my life for seven years, and now I had bumped into reality once again. But this time, reality was there to stay.

I felt disgusted with myself, with my body, and very confused. "Why? *Why?!?*" I asked myself. That I was raped was sad, but true. Now I would have to live with it and deal with it. *But how?* I didn't know how.

When I was released from the Girls Ranch, I turned to drugs. That was the only way I could deal with the pain. Doing crack helped me release my pain, forget the nightmare. When I was using, I would stay up for weeks. I wouldn't have to go to sleep and see that little girl dying.

With the help of Shannon, a strong, supportive, and inspiring "Big Sister" social worker, I realized that life has more meaning than getting high. She helped me believe in myself and put the pain of the nightmare behind me. It's been three years now since I've been out of jail, and I've been off drugs for six months. I'm a seventeen-year-old tenth grader and a single mother of twin girls. I plan to go to college in three years. I want to be a counselor and help teenagers. I want to let them know that drugs are not the only way to escape your pain and problems, and that there is hope out there. I feel good about myself now, even if every night and every day of my life I have to live with the knowledge of the nightmare.

# Childhood Lost

*J.M. Eckrich, age 18*

EVERYWHERE I WENT HE WAS THERE, ASSUMING THE IDENTITY OF an innocent bystander. How could I escape what he did to my mother and me when he was everywhere? Every car I passed driving down the road was him, racing to find me, racing to hurt me, use me as his personal slave. Every person in the store was him watching, waiting.

He was my stepfather. My mother met him shortly after my mother and father went their separate ways. She fell for his apparent kindness and love. She was on her own and felt she needed a man in her life. She did not see the alcohol, drugs, and other vices that lurked in his demonic mind.

I remember seeing her one morning with a pack of ice over the eye where rage had consumed the dirty bastard the night before. I was helpless. He referred to me as his "baby girl" and expected perfection from me. I was expected to act like an adult and take on adult responsibilities, such as cooking, cleaning, laundry, and child care. Often my mother was the only one working, while he sat at home and smoked marijuana.

When I was nine, after many attempts to leave, my mother had had enough and we left. I was so relieved when my mother said we would be going back to her family, about 500 miles away from the scum. After two months, however, his antics once again fooled my mother, and we were back. When we returned, I began playing basketball. He hated all sports and did not want me to play. That made me play even better. Basketball quickly became my outlet. I put my life into basketball.

I was always on my toes, careful not to upset him. I had to comply with his every whim, always pleasing his palate. I was expected to be a genius and to never make any mistakes. Therefore, I excelled in academics to keep him satisfied. No one at school ever knew of the wretched standards I complied with.

The alcohol and drugs heightened his ever-present mental problems. He had several mental breakdowns. Once he believed the devil was in the back of his van and scratched "Free van, Call 666-6666." He used his mental illness as a scapegoat to deal with the world. Although he could have easily controlled it with medications, he never took them. Instead he drank and used drugs.

His final breakdown was a drunken rage against my mother. At the time, she and I had our hair long because that was the way he liked it. After beating her, he cut her braided hair as if it were a trophy. Fleeing for safety, she was forced to leave my brothers and me behind to cope with his irrational thoughts. That was the night I lost my childhood. He touched me in a lewd way, telling me that's what all good daddies do. Lost in emotions of shame and betrayal, I kept my feelings in. I could tell no one; he had promised to kill me if I did.

A week of my seemingly endless shame went by, and another rage was brewing. He was growing more intense every day. On August 7, 1991, near 6:00 P.M., my mother was at work and I was preparing dinner. I knew something very bad was going to happen that night, but I had no control over it. I tried frantically to remain busy and to keep my brothers hidden from the rage welling deep inside the demon.

He ordered my brothers to bed, then he raped me. Not knowing what to do, I screamed and writhed in pain, but nothing could stop this man. I remember the blood all over my legs, the uncontrollable sobs welling up inside me, the passed-out, putrid, naked man. I couldn't handle it and slipped into a different world. Fearful, I waited for my mother to help me. She came like a beacon in the night and rescued me. I was numb and could not comprehend her haste. At the hospital they were disgusted at the damage inflicted, which would require stitches.

It seemed as if it would never end. They expected me to admit I was dirty. I had to testify in court under oath what had happened. I hated myself. I hated everyone. The pain was so deep, so brutal. I was filled with bitterness. But my mother was always there. She took me to a counselor who assisted me through the trial and helped me find the lost little girl. It took years of counseling to help me cope with what happened to me. I was filled with so much contempt that everyone was my enemy. I learned to forgive and to not use sarcasm as a defense. I now have a new life with high goals. I will graduate this year and go to college. I no longer fear the pain of my lost childhood, but anticipate the joy of my adulthood. He is but a memory that no longer follows me on my lifelong journey.

# Death and Dying

# Growing Up without a Dad

*Nicholas Jovän Celestine, age 17*

LIVING IN A SINGLE-PARENT HOME IS HARD. UNFORTUNATELY, many children have to grow up without one of their parents. I live in a single-parent home with my mom. My father died when I was two years old, and growing up without him has been hard. When other kids talk about fathers, I can't help but feel sad. I have no memories of my father, so I cannot relate to their joy. Sometimes late at night, before I go to bed, I think about what life would be like if he were still alive.

I have a small sense of who he was from the stories my mother tells me. I love listening to these stories because I can see parts of myself that I got from him. It is very hard for me when people find out about my father and feel sorry for me. I don't want their pity. I've made it this far without him. I'm not mad at him, though. I can't be. When someone tells me how one of their parents has passed away, I can relate to them. I feel like I have a bond with that person.

I am lucky. I have a great mother who loves and cares for me. I couldn't live without her, and she couldn't live without me. We depend on each other. When I look back on my life, I feel grateful because I have survived. It was hard all those years, suppressing the hidden anger of not having a father; however, I now feel as though it was an obstacle I had to overcome. I am almost a man now. Even though I am still not mature, I have many responsibilities that help me to become more mature. If I ever have children, I only hope that I can be there for them, so they don't have to grow up without a father. Perhaps my loss will be their gain.

# Misdiagnosed

......................................................

*Jessie Dotzler, age 17*

IN MAY OF 1992 MY LIFE WAS TURNED UPSIDE DOWN. I HAD everything: a dad who was always there to help me out in everything I did, a mother who would always sit and listen to me, and a little brat of a sister, Lisa. The perfect family, but how was I to know that four months later it would be gone?

In early May my parents called my sister and me in from outside. We were disappointed because we were having fun. My parents sat us down in the living room. We had no idea what was going on. I thought my grandpa had died, because he was very sick at the time. Instead, they told us that our family doctor in Decorah had misdiagnosed my dad. My dad had had a large mole on his arm, and the family doctor said not to worry, it wasn't cancerous. My mom thought we should get a second opinion, so they went to a doctor in LaCrosse, and that's when my dad was diagnosed with melanoma cancer, one of the worst you can get and one that does not have a cure.

I was in total shock. I couldn't believe it. My sister broke down crying. (She and my dad were very close; wherever he was, she was.) I thought I should stay strong for Lisa and not cry. And I did just that. I put my arm around Lisa and calmed her down. I saw my parents' eyes fill up with tears.

My dad said it wasn't going to change anything. "I'm still going to be the same old guy. I just won't be working. I'm going to stay home with my family."

In early June, about a month later, not one word my dad had said was true. He was in a hospital in LaCrosse, and he could barely sit up in his bed. At this time he was getting chemotherapy, which the doctors said was helping. He got to come home near the end of June. My parents' bedroom turned into a hospital room. It had the bed, the machines, and even the nurses twenty-four hours a day.

During the time he was home, he always wanted someone in his room with him, reading to him. My mom didn't work, and Lisa and I were on summer vacation, so he always had someone. I remember being in there at 2:00 A.M., reading to him about all the cars and trucks that were for sale in the newspaper. He said, "When you turn sixteen, we'll do this again and you can pick out any car you want." It was nice to have my dad home, even though he couldn't get out of bed that often.

In the middle of July things changed. My sister and I went to stay with our grandma and grandpa Dotzler in Ridgeway. It was hard being twelve years old and not being able to go to the pool with friends or ride a bike around town. While staying with my grandparents, my sister and I got very close, almost like friends. We would go see our dad in Decorah about once a week until school started in August.

About two weeks after school began, my dad had to go back to the hospital in LaCrosse. He started chemo again, but this time it didn't help. Lisa and I would stay in LaCrosse for a day or two and then go to school. I hated going to school; all I thought was, "Is my dad okay? Maybe he needs me to read to him now." My dad had seventeen brothers and sisters. They all took turns staying with him. My mom was there every day and every night. They gave her a special room so she could keep all her clothes and things in there and so she would have a place to sleep.

One day, when my sister and I got home from school, my aunt and two uncles were waiting for us. They said we needed to go to LaCrosse. This was unusual because we had been up there all weekend and it was only Tuesday. When we got there, the waiting room was full of relatives. The first thing that came to my mind was that he was gone, but my mom said, "No, we need to talk to you about something."

Then my dad's nurse walked in and knelt in front of Lisa and me and said, "Your dad has a brain tumor, and the cancer has spread so far that there is no way to cure it. Your dad only has about a month to live." My sister and I looked at each other and tears rolled out of our eyes. Could this really happen to my dad? My mom took us in her arms and held us. After we calmed down a little, we went to see my dad. They told us he had changed a lot since we had seen him on Sunday. When Lisa and I walked to the bed, he asked, "Who are you?" My mom told him that these were his two daughters. We reached down to give him a hug. He whispered "I love you." That was the last thing I ever heard my dad say.

Lisa and I went back home. On October 6 we came home from school and my mom was sitting at the kitchen table. She said, "Your dad is gone." We all sat there crying.

I will always remember that night at the hospital and all the fun times we had together. I wish there would have been many more. Hopefully, I will see him again someday.

# My Dad

*L.R., age 17*

WHEN YOU'RE TWELVE YEARS OLD AND YOU DON'T KNOW THAT your dad is going to die in a couple of hours, you think everything is going fine. One event can dramatically change your life forever. You're attending a party that night and trying to get ahold of your dad. You can't, but you're not too worried. He's out on business selling his rugs, making money. My dad was self-employed, and he worked a full-time job on top of that. He made rugs and taught classes on rug making. My dad was a great man whom I loved very much.

January 29, 1992, is a day I will remember for the rest of my life. My dad passed away on that day. I could never have known how it would change my life.

I never liked my dad's side of the family; I always thought they were weird. They were family, though, so I had to be polite to them, which I was. My cousin Crystal and I were very close. She was the only relative on that side that I liked. She was my best friend, and I told her everything. After my dad passed away, his side of the family became very greedy and tried to get whatever they could. It hurt me more than anyone could ever imagine. The only thing I wanted was my dad to be with me, and the only thing they wanted was the money, house, van, business, and everything else that he had left behind.

January 28 was the last time I would ever see my dad. I was happy that my sister and I got to spend time with him. He bought stick-on tattoos and put them all over my sister. It was very funny. We had no idea that anything was wrong with my dad. He didn't like doctors, so he only went when he had to. To this day I have not seen a doctor's report explaining why he passed away.

The next day I had a party to go to and I needed him to pick me up that night. I called him all day long. He was nowhere to be found. I figured that he was out working (because he was always working). I went to the party and my mom said that she would keep trying. When it came time to pick me up, it was my mom. I was surprised. I asked her where dad was, and she said she didn't know. We went grocery shopping and then home. I went right to bed. Half an hour later or so, my mom came up and said "I have something to tell you." She was crying. She said "Honey, your dad died." I immediately thought of my stepdad. My dad was invincible—nothing could ever happen to him. But no, it was my dad. That is when the chaos began.

The funeral came and went. It was nice. Afterward, as I said earlier, my dad's side of the family became bitter and greedy. They wanted everything for themselves. We had to go to court with them. It was very hard telling my grandma that I didn't want anything to do with them. We had to make a decision about moving into my dad's house or not. We tried to sell it, but they (dad's family) stopped the sale of the house. We had a buyer, but they wanted it for my uncle and his family. They took everything out of my dad's house for "safekeeping." Yeah, right. We got everything back except for several thousands of dollars my dad had in a coat pocket. They claimed they didn't see it, they don't know what happened to it.

My cousin and I went to the same school. One day I went up to talk to her and we got into an argument. I said "I am going to lunch." She yelled at me, "We are going to get you!" Not only did that hurt, but it was so embarrassing. We went to court with them— we went to battle and we won. We got to stay in the house and keep the stuff, although we did sell the van and the business because we didn't have time to run the business.

I still have many questions about this story. I don't speak to anyone on my dad's side of the family except Crystal, because we have talked and worked it out. Not having my dad here has left a void in my life. I have learned so much from this experience. I had to grow up before it was time for me to. I had to take care of my sister because my mom's business was failing. I took care of my sister, cleaned the house, helped my sister with her homework, put her to bed, cooked, and woke her up for school. My stepdad said that I was bitter about having to do all that, but I knew I had to do my part after my dad passed away. I will never forget anything that has happened. I will remember how we all had to work together as a family to come out okay. In my opinion, we have done very well.

# My Special Person

*Frances Peña, age 14*

MY STORY IS ABOUT A PERSON I THOUGHT WOULD BE HERE FOR-
ever, a person I thought would never ever leave me or the ones she
loved. But one year, my grandma got sick with pneumonia, and that
was when all of our lives changed for the worst.

February is a month that is supposed to be full of happiness, can-
dies, balloons, and a whole lot of love. All that stuff came and went
but if I could give back all the happiness I had during that last year,
I would. Around the middle of February my grandma fell ill with
pneumonia, and, after that, nothing was the same.

When my grandma was in the hospital it was easy for me to be
there for her. I loved to go visit her. I am the kind of person who can
take going to the hospital, seeing the machines, and smelling all the
medicines. I guess I went enough times for both my mom and me.
Sometimes I would even skip school to stay with my grandma.

My cousins took my grandma being in the hospital harder than I
did. I guess I always believed that she would get better and come home
and that everything would be the same. But, boy, was I wrong! When
my grandma did come home she had machines hooked up to her, and
that scared me. My cousin and my uncle were there all the time. My
grandma needed someone to care for her twenty-four hours a day. My
aunts hired someone to care for her during the week at night.

But Friday and Saturday were up to my cousin and uncle. They
took shifts all night long. The first time I went to my grandma's
house I was scared. I had no idea why, because I had gone so many
times to visit her in the hospital.

When I went to stay with my cousin for the night, she taught me how to suction out my grandma's mouth so she would not have any mucus stuck in her throat. My grandma always made it difficult for me to stay there with her. Whenever I was there, she would ask for my cousin or uncle. By the time I had learned to give her her medicine and all the other care she needed, I was so frustrated with her that I didn't even want to go because she didn't trust me. My family could not understand why I did not want to go and stay with my grandma. It was hard for me to see my cousin so buddy-buddy with my grandma, while my grandma could hardly stand to have me around.

I guess you could say that after my grandma came home we drifted apart. My grandma was a person who knew everything that we did even though she couldn't walk before she had gone into the hospital. My grandma had been handicapped for about fourteen years.

When we got the phone call saying that my grandma was gone, I was asleep. My mom woke me up saying that something was wrong with my grandma and that she was not responding. I told my mom that everything would be okay because my grandma was tough and she knew everything. Well, I was wrong. She did not get through.

The day that my grandma passed away was December 20, 1997. The pain that we felt could not be described.

My grandma was a person who could not get out of bed because of illness and her handicap, but her mind was all there. My grandma was the only one who had remembered my birthday, of all the people who should have forgotten.

I guess you could say that the moral of my "true" story is that you should never take what you have for granted.

# A Piece of Myself

*Heather Reeves, age 16*

You never realize how important someone in your family is to you until they are taken away. On February 1, 1994, I learned how true this is. My world of crystal and sunlight shattered at 9:55 on a Tuesday morning.

It was my seventh grade year at Columbiana Middle School. I was in band getting ready to go to my third period class when I was called to the office. I walked there wondering what it could be that they wanted.

When I got there I saw my older brother Josh in the principal's office, crying. Being the mean sister that I am, I asked him what he had done to get himself into trouble. When Mr. Buck, the assistant principal, came in and asked me to sit down, the look on his face told me he had some bad news. He said that Gabe Hunt, my cousin, who was like my brother, was dead and his little brother Nathan had been in the car when it crashed. These words will remain on my mind and heart for the rest of my life. The pain from that moment I will never forget. Sitting there in that cold office with Josh crying at my side, I longed to be anywhere but there. I wondered if Nathan was going to live and if Laura, my best friend and Gabe's cousin, knew.

Later that night on the way to the hospital, my parents told me Nathan had staples in his head, stitches all over his face, and a cast on his left leg that went all the way to his hip. His mother had not yet told him about Gabe.

When I walked into the lobby of the hospital and saw Laura standing there crying, I knew at that moment our lives would never be the same. I lost a piece of myself that day, and I tried for years to get those pieces back. Now I realize they were washed away like sand on the beach during a storm.

Later that night, after Nathan repeatedly had asked how his brother was but had not gotten an answer, his mother decided to tell him. All he said was, "I'm so sad," and he started to cry.

The day of the viewing, Laura and I went to the funeral home together. We walked in, clutching each other's hands for support and comfort. As we entered the funeral home, the smell of flowers stung my nostrils. The weight of death hung heavily in every corner of the dark room. As soon as I saw the casket, all barriers fell. My heart was in shreds. Laura and I cried in each other's arms. Friends came and offered words of sympathy that did little to give me comfort.

That night, while sitting in bed, I overheard my dad tell my mom how hard it had been for him to tell his sister that her son was dead. My dad, who almost never cried, was crying. And so I cried, too. I wondered how a world could be so cruel. I prayed and asked God why he had to take Gabe away.

The next day the doctors decided to release Nathan so he could attend his brother's burial. While putting him in the car, every movement caused him to scream out in pain. I stood by with tears streaming down my cheeks, wondering why he should have to bear this all alone.

Gabe's funeral was beautiful. So many people came to say good-bye that lines formed outside the chapel just to get in. When they wheeled Nathan in to see his brother, a kind of silence fell over the crowd. Even though he was broken and bruised, he forced himself to stand up so he could tell his brother good-bye. He looked so helpless and hurt.

During the sermon, the preacher read a poem I wrote about Gabe. I did not know till the last minute that they were going to read it. I really do not remember much. It is stored in my memory, locked away to keep me from going insane.

A few days after the funeral, my parents took me to see what was left of Gabe's car. It scared me so bad that I had nightmares for months, and sometimes still do.

Now, almost four years later, I face each day knowing that I have one more angel in heaven looking out for me. Not a day goes by that I don't think about Gabe. I have not yet learned to let go, and I often cry over the words "Gabe's dead." They linger in my dreams and wait in the corners of my mind for me to think back to that terrible day. But I will overcome my pain and I face each day a little stronger, for one day I will see him again.

# The Experience That Changed My Life

......................................................

*Jessica M. Foran, age 16*

JUNE 7, 1995, WAS A DAY THAT CHANGED MY LIFE FOREVER. UP until then, I had lived in a fairy tale. I had a classic storybook family: a loving, hardworking father, a supportive homemaker mother, a brother, a sister, and, of course, a dog. We had a bond so strong I thought it could never break. I was dead wrong.

The details are still burned crystal clear in my memory. I remember looking out the window during class; it was a beautiful Michigan spring day. June 7 was a Wednesday. I loved Wednesdays because I never had homework, I ate dinner at the mall, and then I went to my youth group at church. Around one o'clock that day, out of nowhere, a horrific storm blew up. Thunder boomed and lightning split through the sky. It only lasted about fifteen minutes, then the sun came out again and the birds continued to sing.

After school, my sister Katie and I rode home with our car pool. Katie was overjoyed because she won the election for vice president of her class. She couldn't wait to get home to call our dad because he had helped her write her speech. To celebrate, we stopped at the Dairy Queen and then headed home. As we pulled up to our house, many cars were parked out front, but I didn't think anything of it because we were selling our house at the time. As I got out of the car with my Blizzard, I wondered why my mom and my brother were huddled together with a group of people. My mom was crying. I ran to her and she said that Dad had had a heart attack at work. No one would inform her if he was alive or not. Instantly, my mind said yes, Dad's dead. I threw down my ice cream and ran screaming into the house. My mom followed me into the house and said we were going to the hospital. I followed in a tearful daze.

Apparently, my dad had been exercising on his lunch break, and as he stepped off the treadmill, he toppled over, hit his head, and fell on the floor. Doctors were with him in less than a minute, because the paramedics were located across the hall. They tried everything they could to revive him, but nothing could be done. He died before he hit the ground.

Mom spent some time with him, and then my sister, brother, and I were allowed to see him as well. As I approached my dad, what struck me was his increase in size. Paramedics had pumped so much liquid into him that he weighed 210 pounds instead of his normal 160. His face was purple and contorted. It didn't look like my daddy. I ran from the room, glancing momentarily at the sobbing doctor who had tried to revive him. My brother and mom had talked to my dad twenty minutes before he went down to exercise. The last words exchanged were "I love you."

As soon as we got home, I put aside the pain I was feeling, and my mind clicked into autopilot. I called friends to tell them what had happened and greeted the many who had begun to arrive and console. The news of my dad's death spread like wildfire. Our house, full of boxes ready to move, became the funeral home.

My dad's dad had dropped dead from a heart attack at age forty-nine, so my dad was well aware of the risks. He was in heart attack studies; he exercised and ate healthfully. He had just had his executive physical a couple months before and appeared to be doing really well. Ironically, he died exercising, at age forty-two.

Many people wondered why this tragedy happened. Why did God let this man die? I began to realize that God had a purpose when he took my dad home to be with Him. My dad was pronounced dead at 1:05 P.M., in the middle of that horrific storm that had sprung out of nowhere. The big bold title of the *Detroit Free Press* that day was "HEART STOPPER." He died at the same hospital where he was born. Coincidental? I don't think so.

I had a dream a couple of days after my dad died. I saw him come down and hug me. For a brief moment, the heavy weight of grief was lifted from my chest. Then, as he disappeared, the weight fell down upon me once again. Interestingly, my aunt, who lives 3,000 miles away, had the same dream.

God used my dad's death to have the gospel proclaimed. My family used to pray for all our friends and relatives who didn't know Jesus Christ as their personal savior, that somehow they could hear and receive the gospel. Everyone we prayed for heard the gospel preached at my dad's memorial service. God was really watching out for us. We were supposed to be out of our house in three weeks, but my parents hadn't been able to find the right house to buy. God provided a beautiful new house, and the builder was a Christian who sold the house to my mom at the price she could afford. What a blessing!

Eleven hundred people attended my dad's memorial service. What made me proud was hearing my dad called "a man of integrity," probably the highest and most honored compliment I have ever heard. My dad made sure that we would be taken care of if anything ever happened to him. I miss my dad very much, and I am thankful he had his priorities in order. He put God, my mom, my siblings, and me all before his stressful job as a lawyer. I came to realize that the only way I could deal with the grief and pain was to put my total control and trust in the Lord. He gives me the strength to make it through each day and provides an embrace to comfort me when I'm down. I've learned I can do all things through Christ, who strengthens me. Now both my dads are in heaven.

# Friend of a Lifetime

*Chelsea Couch, age 13*

I FIRST MET ANTOINE MARQUIS ANDREWS WHEN I WAS ABOUT nine years old. We lived in apartment buildings beside each other in Germany. He was a year older than me, but after only a few months, we were best friends and virtually inseparable. We told each other everything and stood up for one another often. He lived by this philosophy: "We only live once, so why mess it all up by getting in trouble? Be careful, but not too careful." He was just the kind of guy who could always make you smile, and he saw the bright side of everything when nobody else did. This school year he would have been a freshman in high school, undoubtedly playing football and making straight As—if he were alive.

One time we were outside on a beautiful, sunny, summer evening. We had been out all day, playing around and swinging on the playground swings. It was starting to get dark, so we lay down to rest a minute. Looking up into the sky, we could see the stars begin to appear. We started talking about our wishes and dreams. "One day, I want to be the happiest little kid ever!" was my wish. But when I asked him what his was, he hesitated for a minute, looked over, and said, "I want to save somebody's life, like the firefighters they always talk about on TV." He explained that he wanted to know what it felt like to save somebody's life, to be a true hero.

Antoine, at the time of his death, was only about thirteen years old. He was killed by a single bullet that penetrated his heart. Antoine's friend had gotten into an argument with a gang member. The guy went and apparently got his whole gang. Antoine decided he couldn't just stand by and let them hurt his friend like that. You see, Antoine and his friend were both African Americans living in what was seen as a white man's community. The gang, being all white themselves, turned the argument into a racial issue, knowing that Antoine and his friend didn't stand a chance against them.

Out of nowhere, one of the gang members pulled out a handgun. I can't begin to imagine the dread Antoine and his friend must have felt at that moment, knowing that with one little jerk of the trigger, they both could die. So many things rushing through your mind at the same moment, your whole life laid out before you like a painting. Death can mean so many different things all at once. The famous literary author Marcus Aurelius once described his thoughts of death as "A release from the impressions of the senses, and from the desires that make up their puppets, and from the vagaries of the mind, and from the hard service of the flesh." I guess the gang member had either no heart or no common sense, because he pulled that trigger, instantly killing Antoine. That one single bullet, no larger than an eye, killed what I see as one of the most loyal friends I shall ever have the opportunity to meet.

Since my family and I had moved away, Antoine and I had been keeping in touch over the phone. One week he didn't call, but I got a letter in the mail. It was from his parents. It didn't have a return address, and I found out later they had moved. The letter was about Antoine and the tragedy that had killed him. In my mind, he was, and still is, God's gift to my childhood. He touched my life so greatly that it's hard to explain in words. With him by my side, I felt like I was capable of anything. I could conquer the world. Being popular was never as important to him as being himself. If somebody came up to him and made a racial slur, Antoine would just stand there and look them in the eye, being proud of who and how he was.

When I heard of his death, I was sad, of course. When he died, he took a piece of my soul with him. It's a tragedy that he had to die, especially that way. Tragedies like this occur all the time, unfortunately. "Tragedy must be something bigger than life, or it would not affect us. In nature the most violent passions are silent; in tragedy they must speak, and speak with dignity too," was how the masterful Lord Chesterfield saw tragedies such as these. Antoine was only trying to help his friend, and he was killed for it. I know that mine wasn't the only life he'd touched over the years. He was a determined, proud, and very promising human being. But what I'm trying to say here is that Antoine was only one person. Thousands of wonderful kids like him die every year from this thing called violence.

I've since lost touch with his family and can only begin to imagine what they must be going through right now.

This is my plea, a plea I'm sending out to every adult in every country and every teenager in every nation around the globe: Please make the extra effort, stop the gangs, and ultimately halt the violence. It would be selfish and conceited of us to even think that the future generation of this world, most of whom haven't even been born yet, won't mind if they don't get a chance to live. They have just as much right as any of us to have a chance at a wonderful life, to be a child, to mess up a few times, to grow up and go on with their lives. It's vitally important that we see and think about them now and in the future, and that we begin setting a better example of what life is really all about.

# The Fine Line between Life and Death

*Amy Leora Farrington, age 16*

"Maybe I'll get my first CPR today," I said jokingly as I did before every ride-along. The excitement of saving someone's life was something I had long dreamed about.

My name is Amy Farrington. I am sixteen years old and am currently in eleventh grade, receiving my education through a Christian home-schooling program. I am also a Medical Explorer for American Medical Response (AMR), the largest ambulance company in the world. The Explorer program allows me to go on ride-alongs as often as I want. I get to help out on the ambulance calls, and being home-schooled gives me the flexibility to work at a volunteer job that I enjoy.

I have taken twelve hours of Cardio-Pulmonary Resuscitation (CPR) training, including CPR for adults, children, and infants. I feel fortunate to have had an instructor who drilled CPR into my head until I was certain that I could perform it anytime, anywhere. If anything, I was prepared to have my first CPR.

I've heard that there are two rules in Emergency Medical Services (EMS), and I've found them to be true. Rule #1 is that people die. Rule #2 is that you can't change Rule #1.

We were all lounging around the station on a lazy Thursday morning. I was riding along on Medic 109 with Paramedic Ken and Emergency Medical Technician (EMT) Dana. It had been a rather slow shift. We'd had only one call, and it was almost noon.

Suddenly, the alert tones went off. "Medic 109, Engine 110, unconscious child."

"I hate these kind of calls," said Ken as we ran out to the ambulance.

We jumped in—Dana was the driver, Ken rode shotgun, and I got into the back. The Mobile Data Terminal (MDT) is a little computer mounted on the dashboard of the ambulance. It is used by the dispatcher to notify the ambulance crew of special directions to the call or important updates about the call. We were told over the MDT that the call was for an unconscious one-month-old infant. Ken hit the "responding" button and we took off, lights and sirens.

The ride to the scene seemed longer than usual. Visions of this unconscious, one-month-old baby boy filled my mind. Across the MDT, the dispatcher told us that there were sounds of a woman yelling in the background. We were racing through traffic, going through red lights and trying our best not to think the worst.

"Amy, can you throw the suction onto the gurney?" Dana asked from the driver's seat.

The suction is used to remove anything obstructing the airway of a patient. I unhooked the portable suction from its chargers and placed it on the gurney next to the airway bag.

"Could you get the infant BVM, too?" requested Dana, as we sped through traffic, siren wailing and lights flashing.

"Got it," I replied as I reached for the infant bag-valve mask (BVM), a piece of equipment used to properly ventilate a patient who is not breathing. I grabbed some gloves, slid them onto my hands, and held on to the BVM.

We arrived within minutes. I opened the back doors of the ambulance and jumped out. I saw the child's father standing outside the apartment. With tears rolling down his face and devastation in his eyes, he pleaded, "Please help my baby, I want my baby!"

I walked inside the sparsely furnished apartment and saw the life-less infant lying on the floor. His mother was standing next to him, being comforted by a friend. Dana took the two women outside so they would not have to witness some of the heartbreaking things done during the desperate attempt to bring a person back to life.

The firefighters arrived and walked into the apartment. Ken placed his stethoscope against the infant's chest and felt for a pulse.

"No pulse, begin CPR!" Ken said, opening his intubation supplies.

One of the firefighters began chest compressions. I handed the BVM to another. He hooked it up to the oxygen and began venti-lating. Dana measured the baby for an oral pharyngeal airway (OPA) and placed it in the baby's mouth. The OPA keeps the tongue from obstructing the patient's airway.

"Amy, can you hook up the monitor?" Ken asked me, as he was preparing to intubate.

I unzipped the side pocket of the heart monitor, got out the pediatric electrodes, snapped colored wires, and placed them on the baby's chest. I was trying my best to stay focused. "White on right, smoke above the fire," I whispered to myself in order to get the electrodes in the right places. I glanced at the screen of the heart monitor and saw the waves being generated by the chest compressions. The baby was so small. His little feet were beginning to turn a bluish-gray color from lack of oxygen. Deep down inside, I think this is when I knew that the baby was beyond saving, but I refused to believe it.

The infant's mother came in from outside and leaned over my shoulder to see her baby. "Is he coming back?" she asked, almost pleading with us to give her some kind of good news. But nobody had to tell her, she knew. "Oh my God, my baby's dead!" The mother once again became hysterical and was taken back outside.

My recurring thought was that we were right in the middle of these parents' worst nightmare. We had not met these people before, but we had suddenly become the most important people in their lives.

I looked up and saw the firefighter who was doing chest compressions glance at me. It looked for a moment as if he had a tear rolling down his face. I also saw Ken intubating the baby. He was placing an endotracheal (ET) tube down the baby's windpipe and into his lungs.

"Stop CPR," Ken commanded in order to get an accurate reading of the heart monitor to tell if there was any kind of electrical activity in the baby's heart.

I looked at the screen of the heart monitor and watched it go flatline.

"Start CPR again," Ken said. He hooked the BVM up to the ET tube and began giving epinephrine and lidocaine in an attempt to restart the infant's heart. The baby was moved onto the gurney and then into the ambulance. I jumped in the back along with Ken and a firefighter, who continued to do chest compressions.

"Amy, I'm going to need you to do some bagging for me," said Ken, handing me the BVM. I took over ventilations while Ken administered a series of heart drugs. CPR was continued during the four-minute trip to the hospital. We arrived at the hospital and were met by the trauma team. The infant was rolled into Trauma 3. After just a few minutes at the hospital, the baby was pronounced dead.

The baby's parents arrived a few minutes later. They were taken into a private room and told of their child's death. Their pain was heard throughout the hospital. The sound of anguish coming from those two young parents is something I will never forget. Their entire world was ripped apart; all their hopes and dreams were erased.

I had an extremely hard time dealing with this call. All that night and the next day my thoughts were continually on the call. A few days later, the baby's obituary was in the newspaper. I cut it out and will keep it so that I will never forget. It's a reminder to me to be thankful for all that I have.

I want to dedicate my life to working in emergency medicine. It's because of my opportunity to be an Explorer that I have decided to work in such a field. I want to make a difference. I want to save some parents the devastation of having their children taken away from them through death. I want to save some children the pain of having a parent die. I won't quit until I can honestly say that I have made a difference. There is a fine line between life and death. This call made me realize just how precious life really is.

# This One's for You, Logan...

*Rachel L. Sorenson, age 17*

PERHAPS A WRITER'S WORST FLAW IS A TENDENCY TO FALL IN LOVE with the sound of words. When your usage of words is determined mostly by sound or feeling, you tend to lose their true meaning in the translation. Sure, such writers can create beautiful poems and stories and fill them to the brim with lyrics of love or hate or mystery, but what is there to stand behind those words when their meaning is empty? These writers create for creation's sake. They are no more than false architects, architects who build for beauty rather than substance. The buildings constructed by these architects may be much admired, but their shine is quick to fade and they soon begin to crumble. True writers must never lose touch with the meaning behind their words.

I once was such a writer. I loved words for their softness, for the emotions their sounds evoked. I created poems and stories based solely upon these feelings and sounds. For the fervent person, they were beautiful pieces of emotion, but to the stoic person—the intellectual—they were empty, frivolous. I had lost the meaning and, therefore, the support of the words. My poems were "nice," but they were nothing more than that.

Once a person reaches such a hollow state, it is difficult for them to leave it. For me, it took just one event—one event that has since changed and altered my whole life, as well as my perception of life. That event was the death of my dear friend, Logan Siebenaler (May 19, 1981–February 17, 1997).

Up until that moment, I'd never had to fully confront the issues of death and mortality. Then, all of a sudden, it was staring me right in the face—in the form of my deceased friend. The impact was tremendous, and although I knew that my other friends were feeling much the same way, I felt alone in my emotional turmoil. What words were there to say? At a time when I needed them the most, my words failed me. Many of my friends were sympathetic to my condition, but it wasn't sympathy that enabled me to see how empty my world of words was, and therefore, how empty my life was becoming. In fact, it was something quite the opposite that opened my eyes so crudely last winter. It was apathy.

Apathy is nothing more than a human's defense against what he or she thinks to be too huge or too horrible to comprehend or understand. In Viktor Frankl's book, *Man's Search for Meaning*, he emphatically describes apathy's play on men's minds in the concentration camps of World War II. Frankl describes apathy as "the blunting of the emotions and the feeling that one could not care anymore. By means of this insensitivity [one has] soon surrounded himself with a very necessary protective shell." And so I constructed my personal "shell" against the world, which I used to keep out everything, good or bad.

When faced with a difficult and entirely new situation, it is easy to fall into apathy—and hard to return from it. For me, it affected everything that I was involved in and everything that I cared for. My schoolwork fell further and further behind as my teachers were unsure if they should give me more leeway to grieve or start enforcing penalties for late work. In the end, each teacher took his or her own approach—some of which worked better than others. I lost interest in my dancing right before our competitive season was about to begin. Even music lost its appeal for me, something which never had happened before, nor has since. Most of all, though, I quit writing. As much as I wanted to, as much as I needed to, the words would not come. I had forgotten their meanings and the softness, the feeling of their sounds. Suddenly, they seemed superficial to me.

For weeks, I spent my free time trying to stay out, to do things, to keep myself busy. Thinking hurt too much, so I avoided thinking at all costs. I couldn't seem to concentrate on anything. I didn't even bother with most of my schoolwork anymore. I didn't care. Nothing held any meaning for me. My words became superficial and so did my world. I had become apathetic.

At night, I lied to myself about my well-being, but at the same time, I knew that I was lying. I knew there were stages of grief that I was supposed to go through, and I told myself that what I was doing and thinking was only natural. Unfortunately, I had forgotten another lesson that Frankl described earlier in his book. It wasn't until I took my former English teacher's advice and reread *Man's Search for Meaning* that I realized what had happened all those months before. Frankl quoted Lessing, who once said, "There are things which must cause you to lose your reason or you have none to lose." He went on to add that "An abnormal reaction to an abnormal situation is normal behavior." Although death is by no means an abnormal situation, it certainly was abnormal in my life. By trying to reason my way through the "normal" grief stages, all I had managed to do was lose my normal reasoning and create an abnormal reaction.

My return from apathy is much harder to explain than my descent into apathy. For the most part, the turning point was when a particular teacher pulled me aside and told me that I was falling much too far behind. Although other teachers had already made the same revelation, it meant more for me to hear it from this man. I had had Mr. Kraftson for two years of Honors Social Studies, and he was the most understanding teacher I had ever had. He seemed to realize everything that an average high school student goes through today, including not-so-average circumstances. From the start, he let me do as I thought I should, but once he saw how dangerously low my grades were becoming, he was very candid with me. For the first time since Logan had died, someone's advice got through to me. Mr. Kraftson's words meant something. I finally realized how important my second semester junior grades were to my future, and I knew that I had to make a choice. I could continue as I was and, most likely, fall short of the requirements for honors classes my senior year—earning my worst grades to date—or I could take responsibility for myself and work with my nose to the grindstone to pull out respectable grades. I chose option two.

For two weeks straight, I did nothing but schoolwork. In one week alone, outside of school hours, I took twelve quizzes, five tests, and wrote six essays. Although I was working in overdrive, I never sacrificed my commitment to quality, and this was what impressed my teachers the most about my effort to redeem my grades. What I regained in those two weeks was more than just responsibility, more than knowledge, and more than the determination and self-respect I had been missing. What I regained in that time was my respect and awe for words—for their meaning and for their greatness. In all the work that I did, writing the essays was the hardest for me, because I had to reteach myself to master my own language. It took a lot of time, effort, frustration, and tears, but in the end, I had successfully begun my journey back into words and back into life. I had overcome my apathy, and in doing so, I had conquered the vacuity of my words, making my life in general more complete.

# Missing Dad

..........................................

*Sheila G., age 13*

EVER SINCE I WAS A SMALL CHILD I HAVE BEEN EXTREMELY CLOSE to my dad. My dad changed jobs to take care of my brother and me when I was three years old. While my older brother was in elementary school, I went everywhere with my dad. He could cheer me up when I was sad, and when I needed advice he would get serious and help me the best he could. So whenever I needed help with something, he was the first person I would go to.

My dad was a custodian at a local church. He had pretty reasonable hours. If he had to take me to daycare or other activities, he rearranged his work schedule and brought me there. The times he needed to go to work, I went with him. I would help him out or sit and play games, waiting for him to finish. He left work every day at 3:00 P.M. to be home by the time my brother got back from school. After school, my dad did some work around the house, helped my brother with his homework, or went outside and played baseball with us. He made dinner five days of the week. While my dad was spending time with us, my mom was at work. My dad did all of this every day of the school year for about ten years.

When my brother got old enough to take care of me after school, my dad started working more hours. My dad called us every day when we got home from school to see how we were doing. He also made an effort to participate in our after-school activities.

In the summer, after getting used to not having either of our parents home during the day, my brother and I really got to know each other. Sure, most of the time we would be with our friends, but when we were both home we got along really well.

We have had a different relationship with each other for the past couple of years. My brother and I talk about friends, but we mainly talk about my dad. I remember one time when my brother said that he loved me; it meant so much to me, because he rarely says that.

When my brother gave up sports in seventh grade, my dad devoted a lot of his free time to helping me with sports. In elementary school I played softball, basketball, and soccer. My dad coached my softball team for four years and my basketball team for two years, and he was an assistant coach for one of my teams for numerous years.

My dad was a star athlete all through high school and college. He was offered a job as a gym teacher, but he wanted to start a family, so he turned it down. He was a great teacher, and I always listened to the tips he offered to help me become a better athlete. It was always a great honor to have him not only as a coach, but also as a dad.

Two summers ago my dad got a disease in his back called meningitis. He went to the hospital and ended up staying a few days. When he came home, he wasn't the same. He needed IVs every day, which meant he would have to sit at home for hours waiting for the medicine to drip into his veins. This prevented him from coming to my softball games, but it didn't stop me from coming home and giving him the play-by-plays. After a month or two, things started to look up again. He was beginning to act like his old self. His IVs were cut down to only a couple of times a week. We started to do things as a family more often.

Everything was going well for a while, until my dad got another illness, only this time in his eyes. The doctors tried many different things to cure him. Nothing worked. His eyesight never got better, it just got worse. He was in and out of work, which meant my mom had to work as much as possible to keep food on the table.

Eventually, my dad said he was feeling better, and I hoped that no more bad things would happen to him. However, in less than a week he was back in the hospital. I kept thinking that nothing worse could possibly happen to him. Was I ever wrong. My dad was diagnosed with cancer in his hand, and it eventually spread all the way to his liver. It could not be cured.

During the next five months, my dad was in the hospital about 60 percent of the time. Each time he came home, I spent as much time with him as possible. I never got used to him going back to the hospital. Every time he had to go back, I would be shocked and worried that he would never get better. I would always say to myself, "He'll be back in a day or two." Sometimes I was right, but not usually. Not too many of my friends realized how serious it was. The friends who did know always listened to me and were very supportive.

During the last couple months, my dad wasn't home for three consecutive days. In all those sixty days, he was barely home for ten days. My mom went to the hospital every day after work to see him. My brother and I went as often as possible. Each time we went, my dad looked different. Some days he looked good and other days not so good. He always told us he was feeling better. I know he was just saying that so we wouldn't worry, but of course we worried. How could we not?

Shortly before my dad came home, his colon was taken out in an emergency operation, which meant he didn't eat anything. After a couple of days he began to look very weak. He was always expressionless. He breathed heavily and barely ever talked.

One day my mom told us that my dad's mom was coming to stay with us until my dad got better. My mom said that grandma would help around the house and be there when we got home from school, but my brother and I didn't want any help from anyone. We felt that we could take care of ourselves.

Finally, what I thought was the best thing to ever happen, happened. My dad came home. A hospital bed was sent with him, along with air tanks. "What are those for?" I wondered. That's when my mom told me there was nothing else the doctors could do to help my dad. I couldn't believe my ears. How can anyone stop treating someone who is still living?

The first couple of days after my dad was home, I would come home from basketball and talk to him about everything I could think of. I could tell he was listening; my mom told me that my dad could still hear me. He just didn't always have anything to say back. After a couple of days went by, he couldn't even respond when I talked to him. I started to avoid being in the room with him. I would go out with friends and talk on the phone as much as possible. It was too hard for me to watch him struggling to breathe and keep his eyes open. I know my mom understood that it was hard for me to see everything that was happening with him. My brother, however, always got mad at me for leaving. He said I should stay at home with Dad. Finally, I started to listen to him and stay home more.

I often think about this one Friday when I wanted to go out with some friends and my mom wouldn't let me go. I was mad at her at the time, but I'm glad now that she didn't let me go, because the next morning my mom woke me up early to tell me the terrible news. My dad had passed away during the night. I couldn't believe it; I thought I was dreaming. I always thought my dad would get better.

After a while I went into my dad's room. He looked so different. He had always had this exciting look in his eyes. It was gone now. All that was left was emptiness.

Someone recently told me that things will get back to normal. How can anyone say that? My life is never going to be normal again. The past thirteen years of my life have been with my dad; that was normal for me. Now that my dad is gone, my life will never be normal. There will always be a piece missing from my life, a piece that I will never forget and never stop loving.

For the past two years, my dad was never not in pain. I am so relieved to know that he is not in any pain up in heaven.

# Our Panel of Judges

## MAYOR SHARON SAYLES BELTON

Mayor Sayles Belton began her public service as a teenager, volunteering at Mount Sinai Hospital in Minneapolis, Minnesota. In college she worked for civil rights, traveling to Jackson, Mississippi, to register voters. As the first African-American president of the Minneapolis City Council, and the first African-American and first female mayor of Minneapolis, Sayles Belton is a powerful role model. In 1997, she was elected to her second four-year term as mayor of Minneapolis.

## MARLY CORNELL

Marly Cornell is a social justice activist, artist, and writer who has worked twenty-four years in health care. Her drawings and paintings have been commissioned by organizations such as Primarily Primates, CEASE, and the Animal Rights Coalition. She has written for various publications, including *The Animal's AGENDA,* where she served for several years as a contributing editor. Ms. Cornell has traveled worldwide to speak at many universities about her work. Currently, she is the chair of the Ethics Committee for the Institute for Chemical Dependency Professionals, a contributor to the Speakers Bureau of the Animal Rights Coalition, and a member of the advisory committee for Fairview Press. Marly lives in St. Louis Park, Minnesota.

## JOHN EDWARDS

John Edwards works for Adoptive Families of America, an organization that deals with child advocacy and adoption issues. A voracious reader and a member of the Fairview Press advisory committee, John lives in St. Paul, Minnesota.

## SENATOR ROD GRAMS

Senator Rod Grams (R-Minnesota) was sworn in as a member of the United States Senate on January 4, 1995. He serves on several Senate committees, and, in 1996, he was appointed by President Clinton to serve as a Congressional Delegate to the 51st Session of the United Nations General Assembly. Prior to his governmental service, Senator Grams spent twenty-three years in the field of television and radio broadcasting.

## LINDA HILLYER

Linda Hillyer is a writer, editor, peer-counselor, and disability activist. She is currently compiling an anthology of personal and creative expression by young people with disabilities, entitled *Listen to Our Stories: Words, Pictures, and Songs by Kids with Disabilities.*

## NKAUJ'LIS LYFOUNG

Nkauj'lis Lyfoung is the Project Coordinator for "Don't Believe the Hype" at Channel 2/17, Twin Cities Public Television. She got her break in the television industry by working on *Kev Koom Siab,* the first Hmong television program produced by PBS. Nkauj'lis is also the co-founder of Pom Siab Hmoob Theatre, the first professional Hmong theatre in the United States, and is an actor, director, and playwright. In 1993, she won an Asian American Academic Achievement Award from her alma mater, the University of Minnesota. Along with performing, writing, and grass-roots organizing, Nkauj'lis has also served on numerous panel discussions and has been a representative to national conferences that deal with youth issues.

## ROSEMARIE J. PARK

Rosemarie Park is an associate professor in Adult Education and Human Resource Development at the University of Minnesota. She trains teachers in adult literacy and English-as-a-Second Language. She works with a variety of health, community, and legal professionals to make sure that what they write is readily understandable to the general public.

## MARK VUKELICH

Mark Vukelich serves as Director of Public Relations for Hospitals at Fairview Health Services. Prior to Fairview, Mark served for nine years as the Director of Public Relations for the Minnesota Medical Association. He created the national award-winning "Stop the Violence" campaign and was instrumental in lobbying for a national television rating system. Prior to his work in health care, Mark worked for Minnesota Governor Al Quie and Minnesota Congressman Vin Weber. He also worked as a radio announcer for Minnesota radio stations WWTC, KCLD, and WHLB. Mark Vukelich lives with his wife and two children in White Bear Township, Minnesota.

## SENATOR PAUL WELLSTONE

Paul David Wellstone is the senior senator from Minnesota (D). After receiving his Ph.D. in Political Science in 1969, he accepted a teaching position at Carleton College in Northfield, Minnesota, where he taught for twenty-one years before being elected to the U.S. Senate in 1990. Senator Wellstone is the only U.S. Senate contender to unseat an incumbent.